RATIONALITY AND MIND IN EARLY BUDDHISM

FRANK J. HOFFMAN

Rationality and Mind in Early Buddhism

MOTILAL BANARSIDASS
Delhi Varanasi Patna Madras

First Published, 1987

MOTILAL BANARSIDASS
Bungalow Road, Jawahar Nagar, Delhi 110 007
Branches
Chowk, Varanasi 221 001
Ashok Rajpath, Patna 800 004
120 Royapettah High Road, Mylapore, Madras 600 004

ISBN: 81-208-0211-X

PRINTED IN INDIA
BY JAINENDRA PRAKASH JAIN AT SHRI JAINENDRA PRESS, A-45 NARAINA INDUSTRIAL AREA, PHASE I, NEW DELHI 110 028 AND PUBLISHED BY NARENDRA PRAKASH JAIN FOR MOTILAL BANARSIDASS, DELHI 110 007.

CONTENTS

DEDICATION

to Leona M. Hoffman

FOREWORD

Dr Hoffman has at his disposal an unusual combination of talents and resources. There are few scholars of Buddhism who have a competence and training in Western philosophical techniques and there are even fewer whose primary background is in Western philosophy who can cope with, let alone discuss, texts in Pali. Frank Hoffman is one of that select band as this book demonstrates. The importance of dialogue between East and West is unquestionable. What is more difficult to achieve is dialogue in depth and with sensitivity. This book achieves precisely that and I commend it warmly.

PROF. STEWART R. SUTHERLAND

University of London,
King's College

PREFACE

'Early Buddhism' is understood in this work as 'the Buddhism of the five *Nikāyas*'. Chapter 1 outlines a method of approach to the study of early Buddhism which is on the interface between Philosophy and Buddhology, but the use of philosophy is not seen as a wholesale imposition of a type of thought as a mold to be set on the Buddhist texts. Instead, attention to Pali language and to some problems of philosophical interest is regarded as jointly useful in making a conceptual map of part of the early Buddhist terrain, and in vigilance for applicable internal and external criticisms.

After arguing against considerations of methodological, logical, and emotive points (in Chapters 1, 2 and 3 respectively) which seek to eliminate inquiry by asserting that early Buddhism is unintelligible or perversely pessimistic, the next three chapters discuss mind. In Ch. 4 a discussion of the terms *citta*, *mano*, and *viññāṇa* is given in section I, and in section II the problem of the compatibility of the 'no soul doctrine' and rebirth, and the problem of the reidentification of persons is discussed. The problem of reidentifying persons across lifetimes cannot be dispelled by appeal to the Buddhist empiricism thesis (Ch. 5). But in rejecting the Buddhist empiricism thesis it is not being suggested that *parinibbāna* is a 'transcendent state', since (with light from Buddhist texts and contemporary philosophy of religion) *parinibbāna* may be understood as 'eternal life' rather than 'endless life' in a way which does not conflict with the 'no soul doctrine'.

The present work is a revised version of my Ph.D. dissertation in the University of London, King's College (1981). Without the Tutorial Studentship in Philosophy of Religion (1979-1981), the dissertation on which this book is based probably would never have been completed. I am therefore grateful to those who provided the award, especially to my supervisor, Professor Stewart R. Sutherland, then Chair of the Department of the History and Philosophy of Religion and now College Principal. One could not hope for a better blend of criticism and kindness in a dissertation supervisor. I would like also to thank my internal examiner in the University of London, Rev. Dr. Michael Simpson (Heythrop College), and my external examiner from the University of Oxford, Professor Pichard Gombrich (Balliol College), for their criticisms and advice. Doing so does not imply, however, that this three-man dissertation committee subscribes to the views presented herein, for which I alone am responsible.

Several scholars of South Asia at the University of Hawaii deserve mention for the outstanding teaching which stimulated and maintained my interest as a graduate student there, especially Profs. Eliot Deutsch, David J. Kalupahana, Prithwish Neogy, Rama Nath Sharma and K.N. Upadhyaya. I must acknowledge the generous assistance of the Department of Philosophy and the Asian Studies Program for teaching assistantships and of the East-West Center for a grant, all of which enabled me to do preparatory studies prior to writing this work.

Finally I would like to thank Mrs. Jean Klemenc for outstanding editorial assistance, and the Research and Special Projects Committee of the University of Montevallo, for a grant provided by the University.

CHAPTER 1

UNDERSTANDING EARLY BUDDHISM

This is a study of the Buddhism of the five *Nikāyas*[1]. For convenience the term 'early Buddhism' is used here as a shorthand for 'the Buddhism of the five *Nikāyas*,' but in so doing it is not being suggested that all parts of the five *Nikāyas*, written in Pāli, are of the same chronological stratum. Scholars concerned with chronology may find reason to believe that even in the same collection or *Nikāya* there are passages comparatively later than the majority in the collection. The possibility of interpolations creeping in cannot be credibly ruled out by asserting dogmatically that the five *Nikāyas* are the very words of Gotama Buddha.

Nevertheless the *Nikāya* literature* is clearly the earliest source material for the study of Buddhism, and is often appealed to by proponents of sects which characteristically focus upon other and later texts. There are various ways of studying Buddhism, both in terms of demarcating which texts to study, and in terms of the discipline primarily used to elucidate them (*e.g.*, philosophy). I make no claim that my procedure is the best or only valid one with which to study Buddhism, but only want to make my particular bias and interest clear at the outset. Agehananda Bharati once remarked on the separation of orientalists and philosophers:[2]

> It is extremely difficult to make them meet, because a lot of cross-disciplinary studies are needed for both—the philosophers will have to read some original tracts of Indian thought in other Asian languages; and the orientalists will have to acquire some knowledge of contemporary philosophy, especially on the terminological side.

My hope is that this work succeeds in getting philosophers and orientalists talking to each other more, counter-acting the narrow-minded prejudice that exists in some quarters on both sides, that they have nothing to say to one another. In my view the study of

*Throughout this work the phrase 'the Nikāya literature' refers to that of the five Nikāyas.

Asian thought is both accurate and non-trivial to the extent that it is both textual and philosophical. Yet this does not mean that the texts have to be strait-jacketed into an alien and perhaps preconceived philosophical framework. An example of this is to be found in Conze's treatment of *dhamma* in a dialectical manner.[3] The trouble is, if one begins with a particular view into which it would be nice if the texts fit, the likelihood is strong that one will end by representing the texts as if they were amenable to an alien mold, or of making baseless assertions.

Some scholars, such as Niels Nielsen, make a distinction which I find useful in beginning to characterize the approach taken in this work. Nielsen (with John Y. Fenton) writes:[4]

> The *emic* (inside) *meaning* of a religious tradition is a description of that tradition by its adherents using their own language and their own categories and systems of organization.... In practice, most investigators use *etic* (outside) *interpretive categories* devised within their scholarly disciplines in addition to emic categories....Emic and etic approaches can be complementary and mutually corrective.

Throughout this work wherever practicable both emic and etic perspectives on an issue are presented. The etic interpretive categories which comprise my frame of reference are taken from philosophy of religion and Buddhist studies.

In this century there has been a movement away from a judgmental Christo-centric point of view in the academic study of religion toward a more descriptive, less obviously biased view. Yet in Pāli Buddhist scholarship there remain apologetical strands, with proponents of, say, empiricism and ecumenism offering various interpretive filters through which to see Buddhism.[5] Although I think that some knowledge of contemporary philosophy is an asset in studying Buddhism, it is not useful in any wholesale way by the imposition of a type of thought as a mold to be set on the Buddhist texts. And there is no suggestion here that any particular philosopher is an *avatāra* of the Buddha Gotama. Philosophical sensitivity may be useful in making a conceptual map of part of the early Buddhist terrain, and in a vigilance as regards both internal and external criticisms which apply to Buddhism. As orientalists so rightly insist, attention to the language (in this case, Pāli) is essential. The intent is to turn away from apologetics as an over-all strategy and back to description with some critical notice, taking understanding as the basic task.

Where occasionally comparisons are made between what the early Buddhist texts say and what philosophy of religion works say, the comparisons are not regarded as valuable somehow for their own sake, nor as causal influence accounts, nor as concealed apologetics to make Buddhism seem respectable (for the view taken is that it *is* respectable), but only for the sake of understanding. If it should turn out that there is some clarity in the Buddhist vision (along with some difficulties), this should not be surprising, nor taken as evidence of apologetic intent. Hence, if the philosophy of religion can aid comparative understanding without doing violence to the texts, the absence of exact Pāli equivalents to its distinctions (*e.g.,* between endless and eternal life as two views of immortality—Ch. 6) will be acceptable as a matter of course.

An underlying assumption of this study is the view that differences between religions are at least as important as similarities. At a sufficiently lofty level of generality various things may be said to be similar. But what one needs to keep in mind is: what is the point in so saying? Ninian Smart's blistering attack on the 'thesis of religious unity' does seem to me clearly on the right track.[6] By contrast, philosophers and religionists have often stressed the importance of unity. F. S. C. Northrop, in *The Meeting of East and West*, holds that philosophical systems have been outmoded by science and that what is needed is a scientifically grounded philosophy *unifying* the world. And more recently some philosophers of religion, such as John Hick, offer a thin-line theism as the solution to the problem of *unity* in the face of religious pluralism. Rather than taking these sorts of approach, the diversity among and competition between different religions might be seen as a sign of great human vitality, rather than as something to be homogenized under the rubrics of positivism and of theism as in Northrop and Hick respectively.*

*In taking this position I do not go so far as to condone violence between members of different religious persuasions as Swinburne seems to do. See Stewart R. Sutherland, *God, Jesus and Belief* (Oxford: Basil Blackwell, 1984), p. 25.

Accordingly, if the differences between religions are instructive, a contextual study (and here the context is a set of texts) is indeed in order. This does not rule out the possibility of criticism, however, as Ch. 1 argues. And a contextual approach may bring to light what, for some, are surprising possibilities of religion. That, for example, there is a religion which does not accept the concept of a Creator God (Pāli: *Issara*) may indeed surprise those accustomed to define religion as belief in God or as man's response to the transcendent. And it would be folly to suggest that early Buddhism is not a religion at all. For it is neither philosophy in the sense of argument and counter-argument (the 'wordy warfare' rejected by the Buddhists), nor some sort of science or magic, and it plays a structurally analogous role in the lives of believers to what we should call religion in the West.

On the view that understanding is basic to the study of religions and philosophical criticism of them is possible, it is neither necessary nor helpful to assume that early Buddhism is either superior or inferior to the later developments in Buddhist tradition as a result of its chronological position. It is as unfounded to assume that the mere fact of the *Nikāya* literature being earlier than other Buddhist works makes them 'more true' as it is to assume that 'truth is an unfolding development' so that the latest Buddhist trend would have the current, but not the final, word.

With the eye of an historian, B.C. Law observes that early Buddhism provides:[7]

> germs of a philosophical system which came to be more logically and consistently systematized later on.

Taken as the historical point that there is indeed continuity and development in the Buddhist tradition, this is surely right. But what is not correct is the suggestion that early Buddhism is less logical and less consistent than later developments. This suggestion would require a detailed demonstration, but it is not clear how it *could* be shown. For the early texts and, for example, the *Abhidhamma* texts are not on the same level, and hence comparison in terms of logic and consistency (characteristics generally ascribed more to the latter) amount to stacking the deck in the following way.[8] It is rather like comparing the *Bible* with the *Summa Theologica,* and then dismissing the former as less logical and consistent.

The view that the early Buddhist texts are insufficient by themselves and must be supplemented by studies of the commentator, Buddhaghosa, has particular appeal in some circles, and seems to be based on the sort of mistaken view held by Law according to which the early Buddhist texts are unsystematic ramblings. The assumption that the texts are insufficient without the commentaries emerges, for example, in a review of A.K. Warder's *Indian Buddhism* in which Alex Wayman writes:[9]

> My own position is that a restriction to either one of the two sides (the scriptures and the commentaries) is structurally convenient for writing a book and not for solving problems: to solve problems one must include all the possible evidence and therefore cannot restrict himself to the scriptures or to the commentaries exclusively.

Just reading the commentaries would, indeed, be peculiar, since they presuppose knowledge of the texts to which they refer. (It is not clear that anyone actually does this, but I leave that point aside.) The converse, however, is not true. For reading early Buddhism without the commentaries enables one to gain an understanding which would not be possible if the commentaries are taken into account. Of course it is possible, alternatively, to gain an understanding of Buddhism by taking *both* the early Buddhist texts and the commentaries into account. One may take the former sort of understanding as valuable without saying that no one should attempt the latter. Whether, therefore, it is a 'restriction' to keep to the early texts and not take into account the commentaries, depends on what kind of understanding is sought for, on what one takes as the problem to be solved. I think that an important kind of understanding about Buddhism is to see what can be said about the early Buddhist view on topics concerning rationality and mind. If this is the problem that one starts with, then not considering the commentaries is certainly not a restriction, but a methodological necessity.

But setting the problem in this way, is what the historical Gotama Buddha actually taught uncovered? It would be naive to rule out the possibility of interpolations having changed the record after all these centuries. From the viewpoint of critical scholarship all one can claim is to be studying a set of very early texts.

Even from a Buddhist viewpoint, however, the historicity of Gotama in particular does not matter much. For the Buddhist path or doctrine does not depend on the historicity of Gotama in the way that Christianity depends on the historicity of Jesus and on his resurrection. Buddhism 'depends on' Gotama in the sense that he is viewed as the turner of the wheel of doctrine in the present eon. But Gotama is not viewed as the first such Buddha, nor the last. He is considered as a torchbearer, not an initiator, and the path or doctrine is viable or obtains regardless of whether a *Tathāgata* appears in a particular age to illuminate it.

Thus, the path or doctrine does not 'depend on' Gotama in the sense that if he had not become a *Buddha* (in this eon 'the Buddha') one could not possibly achieve the highest goal of Buddhist life. Granted that it would be very much more difficult without such a Buddha to show the way, yet the way is *in principle* discoverable by anyone. By contrast, whether as a matter of fact or as a matter of definition of 'Christian', the vast majority of Christians hold that if Jesus were not the Christ and had not redeemed mankind, one could not achieve Christian salvation. The result is that even if someone were to provide new, cogent evidence to show that Gotama did not exist as a historical person at all, such a demonstration would not affect the validity of the path or doctrine at all.

Jesus' existence is logically a pre-condition for his undergoing a resurrection, as Gotama's existence is logically a pre-condition for his becoming a Buddha. Yet whereas if it could be shown that the Biblical Jesus did not exist Christianity would be undermined, if it could be shown that Gotama did not exist, Buddhism would not be undermined. So it is not the historicity of Gotama which supports Buddhism, unlike the situation with Christianity.

It should not, however, be overlooked that it might make some difference in practice to the tenacity with which Buddhists hold their faith if it could be shown that, although Gotama existed, he was an unenlightened charlatan either in reference to his expressed view of enlightenment or according to some supposedly more developed view of what counts as enlightenment (not fully enlightened). In this respect the situation of Buddhism is analogous to the Christian situation, in which Jesus must be seen as the Christ if the religion is going to be viable. Yet there is this difference: that in these cases one is not concerned specifically with the existence, the historicity, of the religious leaders.

For the record, I see no convincing reasons for denying the historicity of Gotama. But as the study concerns a set of texts which would be regarded as Buddhist even if it turned out that there never existed a Gotama, the understanding which this study offers is not contingent on the existence of a particular person.

The overall aim is, in terms of methodology, to eliminate several obstacles which some scholars have thought made an understanding of the content impossible, and in terms of content, to develop an understanding of rationality and mind in early Buddhism. Throughout, I develop the overall argument in such a way as to interest both philosophers and Buddhologists, and it is this approach, just as much as particular conclusions, which marks whatever originality the work may lay claim to. Although there have been other works on the 'psychology' of Pāli Buddhism, there are few if any written by scholars with philosophical training.

This type of work on the interface between the philosophy of religion and Buddhology is a new possibility for religious studies. There has long been critically-oriented writing concerning conceptual difficulties in Christianity, and while the study of Oriental thought was in its infancy in the West, it was important that some scholars took an apologetical stand on behalf of Asian religions in order to stimulate interest in the subject and in order to jolt some out of a Christo-centric complacency. But that time is past. Every year one is inundated with popular books on Asian thought which recapitulate well-worn doctrines in non-technical language with varying degrees of accuracy. There is a need for scholars to do for Buddhism and other religions what philosophers of religion have been doing for Christianity in presenting conceptual problems. What is needed is, on the one hand, sympathetic understanding of what is internally coherent and linguistically precise in the language of the Asian texts studied, and, on the other hand, attention to Asian thought from a critical philosophical point of view. The former alone leads to a head-in-the-sands ostrich attitude characteristic of foolish complacency; the latter alone leads to arrogant misunderstanding.

In this study it is not that philosophy has only an external (etic) and critical function here. It may function in this way (*e.g.*, a difficulty in reidentification of persons is shown), and yet also philosophy may be useful for internal (emic) understanding (*e.g.*, the endless life/eternal life distinction is shown applicable) in a way which elucidates the texts.

It is important to distinguish the approach of the present work from comparative philosophy. Generally (but not, I think, necessarily), comparative philosophy tends toward either apologetics or condescension with reference to one of the things compared.[10] While these attitudes do not in every case preclude understanding, if held at the *outset*, they can take the form of a one-sided selectivity towards the facts which makes understanding difficult or impossible. Comparisons are useful when they enable one to see the subject in a fresh way, without distorting it.[11] Comparisons are occasionally made here, but there is no overall strategy of a comparative sort.

Some have thought that the fourfold logic sometimes employed in early Buddhism is self-contradictory or else unintelligible. If this were so, it would be impossible to begin understanding early Buddhism at all from a Western viewpoint. Ch. 2 examines the fourfold logic and concludes that it is not self-contradictory or senseless, explaining that it is not a specifically formal logical principle but an heuristic one for debate.

Ch. 3 answers the objection that early Buddhism is emotively flawed as Ch. 2 had done for the charge that it is logically flawed. It does so by examining the concept of *dukkha*, which turns out to be a descriptive-cum-evaluative concept and one which provides no support for a view of early Buddhism as 'pessimistic'.

Having argued against considerations of methodological, logical and emotive points (in Chs. 1, 2 and 3 respectively) which seek to cut off further inquiry by asserting that early Buddhism is unintelligible apart from the commentaries, logically unintelligible, or perversely pessimistic, the next three chapters discuss mind. In Ch. 4 a discussion of the terms *citta*, *mano* and *viññāṇa* is given in I, and in II the problem of the compatibility of 'no soul' (*anattā*) doctrine and rebirth and the problem of reidentification of persons is discussed.

In Ch. 5 the concern is with the notion of 'verification' in relation to the early Buddhist rebirth doctrine. Part I discusses *saddhā* (faith, confidence) and II sees *abhiññā* (special sorts of knowledge and powers) in the light of the importance of *saddhā*. On the basis of I and II the Buddhist empiricism thesis is rejected in III.

In Ch. 6 the deathless (*amata*) is explained in such a way as not to conflict with *anattā* doctrine. Views of *nibbāna* are discussed, the distinction between *parinibbāna* and *nibbāna* defended, and *parinibbāna* explained in terms of 'eternal life' but not 'endless life'.

NOTES

[1]*Dīgha, Majjhima, Aṅguttara, Saṃyutta, Khuddaka.*

[2]Agehananda Bharati, *The Tantric Tradition* (London, Rider & Co., 1965), p. 13.

[3]For details see my review of E. Conze, *A Short History of Buddhism* in *Religious Studies*, vol. 16, no. 4 (Dec. 1980), pp. 506-509.

[4]Niels Nielsen (*et al.* eds.), *Religions of the World* (New York: St. Martin's Press, 1983), p. 6.

[5]Examples of these sorts of advocacy may be found in K.N. Jayatilleke and Lyn De Silva.

[6]Ninian Smart, *The Yogi and the Devotee* (London: Allen and Unwin), 1968.

[7]B.C. Law, *History of Pāli Literature*, vol. I (London, 1933), p. 239.

[8]These two are not being compared with respect to authoritativeness, so there is no assumption here that early Buddhism is authoritative and other strands of Buddhism 'heretical'.

[9]Alex Wayman, review of A.K. Warder, *Indian Buddhism* in *Journal of Indian Philosophy* 6, 1978, pp. 415-427.

[10]In his monograph, *Comparative Aesthetics* (University of Hawaii Press), Eliot Deutsch provides three examples of comparative philosophy with reference in each case to shared problems in two different traditions. This is a glimmer of light in the darkness, considering what sometimes counts as 'comparative philosophy'. On the methodological side, however, more needs to be said about whether and how one can identify 'the same problem' in two different traditions.

[11]Elsewhere (*Middle Way*, vol. XI, no. 3, 1976, p. 119) I have made some comparative remarks but qualify them in order to avoid distortion.

CHAPTER 2

RATIONALITY AND LOGIC

In order for an understanding of early Buddhism to take root it is necessary to see that it is neither logically unintelligible nor perversely pessimistic. In this chapter and in the following one respectively these two charges are examined.

The standard method of demonstrating unintelligibility in a system of ideas is to uncover self-contradiction in it. It does not follow from the fact that a system of ideas has no self-contradictory propositions, however, that its basic concepts are intelligible. For example, someone might argue that there is a form of theistic belief which can be stated without self-contradictory propositions, but that the concept of God is itself fundamentally unintelligible. Such an argument might take the form of showing that some of the attributes of God (*e.g.*, omniscience and immutability) are logically incompatible.

The focus of this chapter is on one common charge of unintelligibility which asserts that the third part of early Buddhist fourfold logic is a self-contradiction and that early Buddhists were confused in entertaining it as a logical possibility.* As Staal observes:[1]

> We are often told that Indian philosophers do not accept the law of contradiction. This may well be one of the causes of the neglect of Indian thought by Western philosophers: for nobody desires to study a body of propositions when he is at the same time told that their contradictories may hold as well.

Before turning to a consideration of the fourfold logic in particular, it is appropriate to consider whether there is any general statement concerning self-contradiction to be found in early Buddhism. At *Majjhima Nikāya* I.232 the Pāli reads:[2]

* The discussion which follows is a shortened and slightly revised version of my article, 'Early Buddhist Four Fold Logic' in *Journal of Indian Philosophy*, vol. 10 (1982), pp. 309-337.

> Manasikarohi Aggivessana, manasikaritvā kho Aggivessana byākarohi, na kho te sandhīyati purimena vā pacchimaṁ pacchimena vā purimaṁ.

In *Middle Length Sayings* B. Horner translates this passage as:[3]

> Pay attention, Aggivessana. When you have paid attention, Aggivessana, answer. For your last speech does not agree with your first, nor your first with your last.

The word 'speech' has been supplied by the translator, presumably because the appropriate verb *vadesi* occurs previously as the likely referent of the elliptical construction. The non-agreement in question is thus a non-agreement of utterances. While two psychological states, utterances, sentences, or propositions may in one way or another 'fail to agree', the logical principle of contradiction is formulated by logicians as applying specifically to propositions, rather than to utterances, for example.

Nothing in the text suggests that the sort of lack of agreement in the Pāli is specifically formal logical agreement. And in order to have a point to the effect that there is a formal logical principle of noncontradiction, there would have to be some word comparable to 'proposition' referred to here. Instead one finds that the referent is 'speech'. Thus, I would translate '*na kho te sandhīyati purimena vā pacchimaṁ pacchimena vā purimaṁ*' as 'you do not indeed connect the latter (utterance) with the former (utterance), nor the former with the latter'.

Seeing the Pāli passage in its context may be helpful. Aggivessana states that the five aggregates comprise the self, but also admits that they are impermanent. Gotama Buddha points out that these utterances do not agree with one another. 'But is it fitting', he is depicted as saying, 'to regard that which is impermanent, anguish, liable to change as "This is mine, this am I, this is my self?" And the story continues with Aggivessana's response: 'This is not so, good Gotama.' Since it is included in the meaning of the term 'self' ('*attā*' in Pāli, '*ātman*' in Sanskrit) that it is permanent, for one thing, anything proposed as a 'self' was definitionally disqualified without this characteristic. Hence, Aggivessana's former characterization of what the self is does not cohere with his latter admission of what the term 'attan' means.

At *Majjhima Nikāya* I. 378 there occurs another interesting case, which reads:[4]

> Gahapati gahapati, manasikaritvā kho gahapati byākarohi, na kho te sandhīyati purimena vā pacchimaṁ pacchimena vā purimaṁ. Bhāsitā kho pana te gahapati esā vācā: sacce ahaṁ bhante patiṭṭhāya mantessāmi, hotu no ettha kathāsallāpo ti.

Horner translates this as:[5]

> Householder, householder! Take care how you explain, householder. Your earlier (remarks) do not tally with your later, nor your later with your earlier. And yet these words were spoken by you, householder: 'I revered sir, will speak as one grounded on the truth. Let us have some conversation here.'

Again *sandhīyati* occurs, and this time is translated as 'tally' rather than as 'agree', but unlike in the preceding example, the relationship between consistency and truth is noted: one cannot be speaking in accord with the truth if what one says is inconsistent. Yet it is noteworthy that '*sacca*' (translated as 'truth' above) can mean both 'real' as well as 'true', truth of being or authenticity on the one hand being indicated by the same word as truth of utterance on the other. The last quoted Pāli selection contains an example of the latter usage, and the former is exemplified in such terms as '*saccanāma*', doing justice to one's name, bearing a true name, as said of Gotama Buddha, for example.[6] The idea is plainly one of being true to one's name in the sense of living as one's name implies. For instance, since 'Buddha' means 'enlightened one', the appropriate behaviour is required in order to be *sacchanāma*.[7] Another example of '*sacca*' in the sense of 'truth of utterance', this time from *Saṃyutta Nikāya* (4, XLI VII, 8) runs as follows:

> Sace te bhante purimaṃ saccam pacchimaṃ te micchā sace pana te bhante pacchimaṃ saccaṃ purimaṃ te micchā.

As rendered by C.A.F. Rhys Davids in *Kindred Sayings* this means:[8]

> If, sir, your first assertion was true, your last was false.
> And if your last was true, your first was false.

She translates the assertions as: 'I would have you look, sirs, how straight is this housefather Citta, how guileless is this housefather Citta, how ingenuous is this housefather Citta', and 'I would have you look, sirs, how crooked is this housefather Citta, how crafty, how dishonest is this housefather Citta'. In this context the former is uttered by Nigaṇṭha after Citta states that he does not have faith (*saddhā*) in Gotama's teachings; the latter after Citta clarifies that instead of faith he has knowledge and vision (*jānanto passanto*) of Gotama Buddha's teachings. Nigaṇṭha is evidently not pleased with these teachings.

There is a problem in interpreting '*sacca*' and '*micchā*' if one goes only by the textual references provided for these terms in the Pāli Text Society's dictionary. For while this work lists meanings of 'sacca' supported by textual references which exemplify the dual meanings of truth of being or authenticity as well as truth of utterance, its account of '*micchā*' cites no textual references in which falsity of utterance is meant, despite the fact that 'false' is listed as a possible meaning. Aside from compounds (in which it typically has an ethical slant), the dictionary lists these meanings: 'separate', 'opposite', 'contrary', 'wrongly', 'in a wrong way', 'false'. After 'false' references to *Sutta Nipāta* verses 438 and 815 are given, but these in fact have to do with *living wrongly* from the early Buddhist viewpoint ('*micchāladdho*' and '*micchā*' being used to condemn pride and lechery respectively), rather than with falsehood as a property of utterances.[9] The last passage quoted above (*KS*, p. 207) might well have been cited as a usage of '*micchā*' as a property of utterances.

In addition to its application to speech or utterances, '*micchā*' is also applied to *diṭṭhi* (views or speculative views, depending on context), and to *saṅkappa* (intentional thoughts), for example. Of course right and wrong are opposites just as true and false are, and a justification for holding that '*micchā*' means 'wrong' sometimes and not always 'false' (contra *PTS dictionary*) consists in the fact that, *e.g.*, '*sammāvācā*' is used as right view in contrast to wrong view.

It is also important to notice that there are terms to mark a distinction between 'intentional thoughts' and 'utterances' ('*saṅkappa*' and '*vācā*'). Hence it is not plausible to argue that there is no rough linguistic basis for a distinction between propositions and speech and that if there had been one, the early Buddhist view *would have been* a view about propositions. If there had been any interest to state a formal logical principle and use a notion of proposition, this could have been done. In fact, I find no occurrences in early Buddhism of the terms for proposition listed in A.P. Buddhadatta's *English-Pāli Dictionary viz., kattukamyatāñāpana, pakāsana,* and *mūladhamma.*

Utterances, unlike propositions or thoughts, may be soft or loud, said in haste or in a drawl, made in a cubicle or in a theatre at a certain time, *etc.* whereas none of these are true of propositions or of thoughts in the same sense. But in saying this it is not being suggested that propositions or thoughts inhabit a ghostly realm somewhere, nor that early Buddhism offers a theory or a technical distinction between thoughts and utterances. But had this technical distinction been important, appropriate terminology could have been devised. In fact, many such theoretical concerns are unimportant from within the context of liberation-oriented early Buddhism.

Philosophers will notice that articulating the distinction between propositions and thoughts, on the one hand, and utterances, on the other, may well hide a dualist snare, and rather than risking a fall into it, it is preferable just to say that different things may be truly said of the one which are not true of the other.

I do not find Jayatilleke clear on the relationship between propositions and utterances. And he is not very clear about whether early Buddhism in fact contains a formal statement of the principle of Contradiction, or just that here we come very close to a formal statement of the principle.

At one point he states:[10]

> Citta is anxious to show that Nigaṇṭha Nāttaputta is contradicting himself and says, sace purimaṃ saccaṃ pacchimaṃ te micchā, sace pacchimaṃ saccaṃ purimaṃ te micchā, i.e. if your former statement (p) is true, your latter statement ($\sim$p) is false and if your latter

> statement ($\sim$p) is true, your former statement (p) is false. In other words, in the above situation when the statements are of the form $\sim$p and p, it cannot be the case that both p and $\sim$p are true ($\sim$(p. $\sim$p), which is the formal statement of the principle of Contradiction.

In order for Jayatilleke's interpretation above to work, however, his word 'statement' must be construed as 'proposition' (rather than as 'utterance'), but in that sense there is no referent in the Pāli passage. The text makes it clear that it is *utterances* which are the foci of attention (not thoughts or propositions), and by using p and $\sim$p as signs for propositions, Jayatilleke is led to the mistaken conclusion that the text gives a 'formal statement of the principle of Contradiction'. By using the words '*bhāsitaṃ*' ('saying') and '*etad avoca*' ('this said'), the text makes it perfectly clear that the former and latter, the *purimaṃ* and *pacchimaṃ*, which contradict one another are utterances. Other examples bear this out as well, and I have found no counter-evidence in the five *Nikāyas*. Thus I conclude that Jayatilleke's interpretation above is mistaken.

In early Buddhism views, thoughts, and utterances may or may not be false as distinct from whether or not they are wrong, and when the early exclusion of self-contradiction is formulated, it is clear that it is not formulated as a formal logical point but one about utterances. Perhaps if there *had* been a concern to make a point about proposition, the word '*vāda*' could have been used, yet it is often translated as 'speech' and only in its usage as 'view', 'doctrine', or 'belief' is there any approximation to 'proposition', and even here it is not close. For in this sense it means 'emphatic or formulated speech' in the sense of 'doctrine'. The fact is that there is no early Buddhist term which might be translated as 'proposition' without a good deal of extrapolation. There is a term for 'wrong speech' and 'lie', however ('*musāvāda*'), so that 'false speech' ('*micchāvāda*') is distinguishable from 'wrong speech' ('*musāvāda*' in the first of two meanings just mentioned).

'*Micchā*' is applied to views (*diṭṭhi*), thoughts (*saṅkappa*) and utterances (*vācā*), meaning 'false view', 'false conception', 'false speech' respectively, according to a translation by Horner.[11] Thus, in early Buddhism a distinction is evident between false utterances or speech, on the one hand, and wrong utterances or speech and lies, on the other hand, so that it is clear in the passage cited that the focus is on truth and falsity rather than on rightness and wrongness. When applied to utterances, '*sacca*' and '*micchā*' mean 'true' and 'false' respectively, unlike '*sammā*' and '*musā*' which in this application mean 'right' and 'wrong' respectively.

But if, as is argued here, the principle of contradiction is not a formal logical principle in early Buddhism, what sort of principle is it? The interpretation which I would like to suggest is that, in keeping with the long tradition of debate which has flourished in India since pre-Buddhistic times, the status of the principle of contradiction can best be understood as that of a rule for discussion.

It is of course obvious that any system of linguistic symbols that communicate information will, *qua* system, *have* an informal logic. Only, it cannot be concluded that the early Buddhist texts *put forth* the principle of contradiction as a rule in informal logic, since they recognized no distinction between formal and informal logic, and since to see oneself as putting forth the latter one must know what counts as the former. But from a later and external point of view one may describe the concern as 'informal logic'. I would prefer to say that they had, and saw themselves as having, an heuristic principle for debate.[12] It is an heuristic principle in the sense of being a *principle of method* on the basis of which one can *discover* things: without it, one cannot find out, discover, or establish anything at all.

When the householder, Upāli, violates this rule (in the example previously quoted), Gotama Buddha perceptively points out the inconsistency of his doing so with his claim to be speaking in accordance with the truth, thus illustrating the considerable importance to be attached to this rule. The consequence of violating the heuristic principle of noncontradiction is that one thereby relinquishes any claim to be saying something that is true.

A different sort of consequence (or putative consequence), one which is mythologically articulated, obtains when the rule is violated that in discussion a legitimate question should be answered at least on its third repetition. The penalty mentioned for this violation is having a thunderbolt bearing *yakkha* (identified with Indra) shatter one's skull into seven pieces![13] We are told that the same Aggivessana who violated the rule of contradiction almost violates the latter rule about answering as well, barely averting his doom by answering after the second repetition while the fiery thunderbolt is overhead. In early Buddhism these rules were powerful weapons against ignorance masquerading as knowledge.

Aside from the exegetical line of argument already given for the thesis, *contra* Jayatilleke, that the early Buddhist principle of contradiction is an heuristic rather than a formal logical one, another line of argument is possible on historical grounds. The exegetical argument shows that in early Buddhism noncontradiction is simply a basic rule for debate, there being here no concern for propositions and logic. The historical point can also be made that there is no evidence of a concern for formal logic and propositions in any school of thought in India at the time of the Buddha.

In his chart on the development of Indian logic, Staal lists the work of Kaṇāda in the first century A.D. as the first to be done on logic in a narrow sense. Staal himself opts for such a broad sense of 'logic', however, (congruent with his sweeping claim: 'the history of Indian logic covers at least 23 centuries...') that the distinctions between logic, grammar, and ritual become blurred.[14] It is important to specify, however, that formal logic plays no role in early Buddhism.

At this point it is appropriate to return to the problem of interpreting the 'both X and not X' part of the fourfold logic. In view of the clear occurrence of the heuristic principle of contradiction that I have shown to pertain to utterances, it would be inconsistent if the third part of the often-used fourfold formula should turn out to violate that very principle. (It is beside the point that Gotama does not urge acceptance of the third lemma in particular, for if early Buddhism considers a self-contradiction as a possibility, then it is fundamentally mistaken.)

Since the literal translation of the third part of the fourfold logic is senseless, the question arises: is there any non-literal but textually consistent interpretation of the third position that makes sense in the early context. One item of internal evidence supporting the contention that either the third or the fourth position does not mean what a literal translation conveys is that on a literal rendering they are semantically equivalent. Although the early Buddhist viewpoint does not include a formal logic, the following formal *parallel* may be constructed in order to demonstrate semantic equivalence.* Taking p and $\sim p$ as parallel to the third position and $\sim(p \wedge \sim p)$ as parallel to the fourth position:

$$\sim(p \wedge \sim p) \equiv \sim p \wedge \sim \sim p \equiv p \wedge \sim p.$$

But if this is the case, then both the third position and the fourth are self-contradictory, and the two self-contradictions are semantically equivalent as nugatory. Yet since the early Buddhist perspective recognizes the two as distinct views, the formal symbolism above cannot be an accurate rendering. Hence, my strategy is to offer an alternative model for understanding the fourfold pattern.

To begin with there are some points about the Pāli which need to be kept in mind for a clearer view of the matter. There are passages which indicate that the fourth, 'neither..nor', is literally meant as in the *Saṃyutta Nikāya* (Pāli Text Society edition, II, pp. 19-20) lines:

7 Kim nu kho bho Gotama sayaṃkataṃ dukkhanti
Mā hevaṃ Kassapāti Bhagavā avoca
8 Kim pana bho Gotama paraṃkataṃ dukkhanti
Mā hevaṃ Kassapāti Bhagavā avoca
9 Kim nu kho bho Gotama sayaṃkatañca paraṃkatañca dukkhanti
Mā hevaṃ Kassapāti Bhagavā avoca
10 Kim pana bho Gotama asayaṃ-kāram aparaṃ-kāram adhicca samuppannaṃ dukkhanti
Mā hevaṃ Kassapāti Bhagavā avoca

The Pāli Text Society translation of the passage is:[15]

7 'Now then, Master Gotama, is suffering wrought by one's self?'
'Not so verily, Kassapa', said the Exalted One.
8 'What then, Master Gotama, is one's suffering wrought by another?'
'Not so verily, Kassapa,' said the Exalted One.
9 'What then, Master Gotama, is suffering wrought both by one's self and by another?'
'Not so verily, Kassapa,' said the Exalted One.

*I have benefitted by discussing this point with Prof. Steve Satris.

10 'What then, Master Gotama, has (the) suffering [which is] wrought neither by myself nor by another, befallen me by chance?'

'Not so verily, Kassapa,' said the Exalted One.

As an aside it should be noted that the phrase '*kim nu kho*' in line 9 has been translated in the same way as '*kim pana bho*' in lines 8 and 10 due to an oversight. It should be translated as in line 7 to convey the parallelism of the Pāli verse. Also, the term '*bho*' has a familiar tone (vocative of the formal '*bhavant*' meaning 'sir' or 'lord'), and was much used by the brahmans as a form of address for equals or inferiors. Hence they are called '*bhovādins*'.[16] The term '*bho*' is rendered by the translator as 'Master' in an attempt to approximate the mild condescension or familiarity of '*bho*' in this context, and should not be thought of as 'Master' in the sense of teacher. Thirdly, the words '*mā h'evam*' which report the Buddha's attitude above do not indicate a simple denial, but rather a prohibition. 'Do not say so' is thus an appropriate translation, as Kalupahana points out.[17]

'*Adhicca samuppannaṃ*' means 'uncaused, sprung into existence without a cause', so that in the above passage the fourth position represents a rejection of the self-caused/other-caused dichotomy altogether, as the phraseology of '*asayaṃ-kāraṃ*' (not self-caused) and '*aparaṃ-kāraṃ*' (not other-caused) indicates. Thus, if the fourth position is literally interpreted (e.g., 10 above as referring to 7 and 8), it makes sense as a rejection of the first and second as offering an overly simple dichotomy. But as previously shown, the third and fourth cannot both be interpreted literally unless the unpalatable consequence of their equivalence is admitted. Consequently the question arises as to whether and how the third position can be given a non-literal interpretation.

As a starting point recall Jayatilleke's interpretations of two Pāli phrases as 'he is semiconscious' and 'the universe is finite (in some dimensions) and infinite (in other dimensions)' presented previously. On this view the third position is a qualified assertion, intermediate between the first and the second, and a tacit convention operates such that statements in the fourfold logic of the form 'both X and not X' are elliptical, leaving out 'in part' after each X. On the basis of the preceding considerations the following schema may be constructed:

(1) there exists an X such that characteristic y applies;
(2) there exists an X such that y does not, but z does, apply;
(3) there exists an X such that both y and z apply in part;
(4) there exists an X such that neither y nor z apply.

In 10 already mentioned it is 'chance' which is the reason given why a position of type (4) applies. The Buddha is depicted as rejecting attempts to involve him in speculative philosophical arguments, saying that he does not hold any alternative fourth position.[18] And the fourth is explained with reference to one who is 'addicted to logic and reasoning'.[19]

Since a wide variety of fourfold examples occur in Pāli, it may not always be easy to see how a given example could admit of the third alternative, which requires distinguishable parts. Some of the examples used are: X understands, X exists, X is pleasing, X expects, in cases where each X has a fourfold pattern of possibilities.[20] Understanding is the sort of thing that one might have in part, and if X is pleasing it need not be completely so. Yet it may be more difficult to see whether and how one can have a 'partial expectation'. (Perhaps one can, as in: 'I rather thought he would come home on time, but was not very surprised when he did not'.) But what of the possibility that X may exist in part? In the context X is the *tathāgata*, and it is not absurd to suppose that some non-Buddhists took it (wrongly) that the Buddhist view is that in the case of the *tathāgata* part of what might generally be called mind (*mano*) continues to exist after death, and part does not. Gotama Buddha clearly is shown to reject this view in chastizing Sati for holding that Buddha teaches that *viññāṇa* ('consciousness') continues after death. I suggest that (3) as applied to the *tathāgata* may be understood as the view that part of the *tathāgata* survives death and part does not. If the part which was thought to survive (*e.g., viññāṇa*) is taken as a sort of permanent *ātman* surrogate, then it is obvious why the Buddha would not hold such a view, since the *anātmavāda* clearly precludes it.

The muddle of regarding the third and fourth positions as self-contradictory and equally meaningless results from taking them as formally symbolized: $p, \sim p, p \wedge \sim p, \sim(p \wedge \sim p)$. Instead I think they can be understood properly as existential statements *viz.*, there exists an X such that y obtains, there exists an X such that y does not obtain but z obtains, there exists an X such that y obtains (in part) and z obtains (in part), there exists an X such that neither y nor z obtains.

Taking a wide range of examples and trying not to be one-sidedly selective, I nevertheless find that the instances of the fourfold pattern in early Buddhism fit this model. For instance, *dukkha* is self-caused, *dukkha* is not self-caused but other-caused, *dukkha* is both self-caused (in part) and other-caused (in part), *dukkha* is neither self-caused nor other-caused (but arises by chance).

Is there any evidence that the fourfold pattern is regarded as exhaustive of the possibilities on the questions to which it is applied? For example, consider this passage from the *Dīgha Nikāya*:[21]

> Ime kho te, bhikkhave, samaṇa-brāhmaṇā amarā-vikkhepikā tattha tattha pañhaṃ puṭṭhā samānā vācā-vikkhepaṃ āpajjanti amarā-vikkhepam catuhi vatthūhi. Ye hi keci, bhikkhave, samaṇāvā brāhmaṇā vā amarā-vikkhepikā tattha tattha pañhaṃ puṭṭhā samānā vācā-vikkhepaṃ āpajjanti amarā-vikkhepam, sabbe te imeh' eva catuhi vatthūhi etesaṃ vā añña-tarena, n'atthi ito bahiddhā.

T.W. Rhys Davids translates the passage as:[22]

> These, brethren, are those recluses and Brahmans who wriggle like eels; and who, when a question is put to them on this or that, resort to equivocation, to eel-wriggling; and that in four ways, or in one or other of the same; there is no other way in which they do so.

Hence a special concern is the force of 'they do so in these four ways...there is no other way in whcih they do so'. Is this a contingent, historical fact that there happened to be four possibilities, or is it more than that—a rule for discussion to the effect that no more than the four possibilities were admissible? If interpreted in the latter way, the passage above is evidence in favor of Jayatilleke's view that the fourfold pattern was taken as exhaustive of the possibilities.

It is interesting to notice that the fourfold pattern is not always applied to debates in early Buddhism, and it might be thought that this is something odd or perhaps even inconsistent about early Buddhism. I do not think so, for understood in the way I suggest, something quite similar happens in other contexts in which there is no possible suggestion of an inscrutable 'Asian logic' at work. A notable example occurs in Hume's *Dialogues,* in which Philo lists four hypotheses on the nature of first causes:[23]

> *that* they are endowed with perfect goodness, *that* they have perfect malice, *that* they are opposite and have both goodness and malice, *that* they have neither goodness nor malice.

Of course no one would suggest that Hume ought always to use this fourfold pattern, nor that he is an Asian logician. Whether one uses the fourfold pattern depends on the issue and on the way one chooses to analyze it.

Whereas Jayatilleke thought the fourfold pattern to be a kind of logic superior to Aristotelian logic, I do not think that this comparison is adequate.[24] There is nothing in the fourfold logic, properly understood, which is either in conflict with, or in advance of, Aristotelian logic.

The main tasks completed here are those of clarifying the status of the early Buddhist principle of contradiction, and explaining how it is compatible with the third and fourth position of the fourfold logic. I have undertaken this task after finding various inadequacies in several accounts of the fourfold pattern. And now it is appropriate to summarize the main findings:

(1) in early Buddhism there is a distinction between 'truth of being' and 'truth of utterance';
(2) '*micchā*' is used in the latter sense in the formulation of the principle of contradiction (or noncontradiction);
(3) there is no word for 'proposition' in early Buddhism, and hence no concern with formal logic;
(4) thus, *contra* Jayatilleke, there is no formal logical principle of contradiction in early Buddhism, but rather an heuristic principle or rule for conducting discussions which makes self-contradictory utterances

illicit. If one calls it informal logic, that is only from an external point of view.

(5) the fourfold logic is best understood as having the general form: 1) there exists an X such that characteristic y applies to it, 2) there exists an X such that y does not apply but z applies, 3) there exists an X such that y applies (in part) and z applies (in part), and 4) there exists an X such that neither y nor z apply;

(6) on this account the third position of the fourfold logic does not violate the heuristic principle of contradiction, and thus there is no internal inconsistency;

(7) on this account the fourth position indicates that some other state of affairs (not any of the preceding three) apply;

(8) finally, the two views that Buddhism has an entirely different kind of logic from Western logic and that Buddhism is fundamentally confused in admitting self-contradictions as valid are both exposed as inapplicable to early Buddhism. Thus, the impossibility of understanding early Buddhism by such appeals is clear.

Throughout I have been concerned to look at early Buddhism in its own terms. When looked at in its own terms, one sees neither fundamental confusion cause for despair (Poussin: 'We are helpless'), nor a modern system of logic constructed in antiquity (Jayatilleke: 'the early Buddhist conception of logic was far in advance of its time').[25] In general a moral to be drawn is that in understanding an ancient world-view, as in understanding a primitive society, it is not necessary that the others be seen as having precisely our concerns in order to be saying or doing something significant.[26]

NOTES

[1]J.F. Staal, 'Negation and the law of contradiction in Indian thought' in *Bulletin of the School of Oriental and African Studies* 25 (1962), pp. 52-53.

[2]V. Trenckner (ed.), *Majjhima-Nikāya* (London: Luzac and Co. for the Pāli Text Society, 1964), vol. I, p. 232.

[3]I. B. Horner (ed.), *Middle Length Sayings* (London: Luzac and Co. for the Pāli Text Society, 1967), vol. I, p. 285.

[4]Trenckner, *op. cit.* p. 378.

[5]Horner, *op. cit.* vol. II, p. 43.

[6]T. W. Rhys Davids and William Stede, *The Pāli Text Society's Pāli-English Dictionary* (London: Pali Text Society, 1972), p. 668.

[7]The claim is that behavior is the criterion for identifying the states of consciousness of others, but not that states of consciousness are identical with behavior.

[8]F. L. Woodward (ed.), *The Book of the Kindred Sayings* (London: Pāli Text Society, 1980) vol. IV, p. 207. This is incorrectly cited (due to typographical error) as p. 270 in my article, 'Early Buddhist Four-fold Logic' in *Journal of Indian Philosophy* 10 (1982), p. 326.

[9]Lord Chalmers, *Buddha's Teachings* being the *Sutta-Nipāta* or Discourse Collection (Cambridge, Mass. and London: Harvard Oriental Series, 1932).

[10]K. N. Jayatilleke, *Early Buddhist Theory of Knowledge* (London: Allen and Unwin, 1963), p. 334.

[11]Horner, *op. cit.* vol. II, p. 71.

[12]A relevant sense of 'heuristic' is given in *A Supplement to the Oxford English Dictionary* II, H-N (1976) as 'a rule or item of information used in such a process' of decision making (B 1 b).

[13]Horner, *op. cit.* vol. I, p. 285.

[14]J.F. Staal, 'Indian Logic' section of 'Logic, History of' in *Encyclopedia of Philosophy* vol. 4 (New York: Macmillan, 1967), pp. 520-523.

[15]Mrs. Rhys Davids and F.L. Woodward (eds.), *The Book of the Kindred Sayings* (London: Pāli Text Society, 1922), vol. II, p. 15.

[16]T. W. Rhys Davids and William Stede, *op. cit.* p. 509.

[17]David J. Kalupahana, *Causality: The Central Philosophy of Buddhism* (Honolulu: University Press of Hawaii, 1975), p. 143.

[18]Horner, *op. cit.* vol. II, p. 177.

[19]T. W. Rhys Davids (ed.), *Dialogues of the Buddha Part I* (London: Pāli Text Society, 1899), vol. II, p. 36. Sacred books of the Buddhists Series, F. Max Muller (series ed.), reprinted in 1977.

[20]Horner, *op. cit.* vol. II, p. 97; vol. II, pp. 177-178; vol. III, p. 184.

[21]T. W. Rhys Davids (ed.), *Dīgha-Nikāya* (London: Pāli Text Society, 1890), vol. I, p. 126.

[22]T. W. Rhys Davids, *op. cit.* (1899), p. 40.

[23]David Hume, *Dialogues Concerning Natural Religion* (Edinburg, 1957), Norman Kemp Smith edition, p. 212.

[24]K. N. Jayatilleke, *The Message of the Buddha* (London: Allen and Unwin, 1975), pp. 49 and 51.

[25]Jayatilleke, *op. cit.* (1975) p. 51; Poussin quoted in Jayatilleke, *op. cit.* (1963), p. 333.

[26]In drawing this moral I find inspiration in Peter Winch's article, 'Understanding a Primitive Society' in Bryan R. Wilson (ed.), *Rationality* (Oxford: Basil Blackwell, 1977), pp. 78-111.

CHAPTER 3

RATIONALITY AND PESSIMISM

Aside from the challenge to early Buddhism on the grounds of fundamental unintelligibility which was examined in chapter 2, another sort of objection comes from those who regard it as wholly pessimistic and in that way 'irrational'. Commenting on this sort of objection E.J. Thomas writes:[1]

> It is not more pessimistic than other religions that have called life a vale of tears, and it is definitely optimistic in teaching that the cause of pain can be known, and that there is a way by which it can be removed. But in being pessimistic it is consistently so, and it requires that one who really knows that existence is pain shall devote all his efforts to stopping it, that is, to understand what the cause is, and then to remove himself from all contact with it. The ordinary man does not believe that existence is pain. Even when he despairs about ever attaining pleasurable ends, he is still under the impulse, the thirst for pleasure. Evidently such a one is incapable of admitting or understanding even the first Truth. He can only come to realize the Truths by a course of moral and intellectual training.

The answer to the charge of pessimism can only be given after some account of the meaning of dukkha and of the claim 'all is dukkha' have been presented. Then after dealing with the problem of whether or not early Buddhism is 'pessimistic', I propose to examine the issue of the nature of pessimism. Are there features of Buddhism, which exclude or render implausible an interpretation of Buddhism as pessimistic? This is the question to be addressed in the present chapter.

We are told that, unlike the ten questions (containing the tetralemma concerning the *tathāgata*) which have not been 'determined' ('*abyākata*' or '*avyākata*' in Pāli), *dukkha* has been determined by him.[2] And in view of its prominence in the first *ariyasacca* or 'noble truth', the concept of *dukkha* is so fundamentally important that it is worthwhile spending some time getting clear on just what has been determined. What is *dukkha*?

To begin with, it is noteworthy that the five aggregates which constitute personality are impermanent, and that whatever is impermanent is *dukkha*.[3] And we find statements like 'formerly as well as now all these material shapes are impermanent, painful, liable to alternation.'[4] While not being synonymous with 'impermanence' ('*anicca*'), *dukkha* thus has descriptive import (a) by virtue of the fact of change in the world. And as the following passage bears out, it also has descriptive import (b) in reference to a range of experience which is minimally that of deprivation, and which may be that of mental and/or physical pain of various sorts:[5]

> Katamañ c' āvuso, dukkhaṁ ariyasaccaṁ—Jāti pi dukkhā, jarā pi dukkhā, maraṇam pi dukkhaṁ, sokaparidevadukkhadomanassupāyāsā pi dukkhā. Yam p' icchaṁ na labhati, tam pi dukkhaṁ; saṁkhittena pañcupādānakkhandhā dukkhā.

A translation by I.B. Horner goes:[6]

> And what, your reverences, is the ariyan truth of anguish? Birth is anguish and ageing is anguish and dying is anguish; and grief, sorrow, suffering, misery and despair are anguish. And not getting what one desires, that too is anguish. In brief, the five groups of grasping are anguish.

Here '*dukkha*' is translated by Horner as 'suffering' in its occurrence in the long and much used phrase beginning with '*soka*' ('grief'), while it is translated as 'anguish' in the other occurrences here. The passage characterizes *dukkha* in the primary sense in which it functions in the first noble truth in terms of several other concepts, among which *dukkha* occurs again (consider the primary sense as $dukkha_1$ and the other as $dukkha_2$). Apparently $dukkha_1$ is not semantically equivalent to $dukkha_2$, for otherwise the characterization would be at that point tautologous.

Although it is disputable whether the former should be rendered as 'anguish' and the latter as 'suffering', Horner has seen the importance of assigning *different* meanings to them. T.W. Rhys Davids and Wm. Stede think that *dukkha* is 'to be understood as physical pain' in the combination of this term and *domanassa*, and render the '*soka* phrase' as 'grief and sorrow, afflictions of pain & misery, i.e. all kinds of misery'.[7] However one interprets the precise meaning of *dukkha*$_2$, the important point to note is that the above passage shows that *dukkha*$_1$, has the much wider meaning indicated at (b) above.

One of the 'eighteen mental ranges' that a monk might achieve concerns *dukkha.* In achieving this mental range a monk 'ranges over the mental state that gives rise to sorrow.'[8] The mental state which gives rise to sorrow is described elsewhere as the 'root of *dukkha*' which, when uprooted stops rebirth[9]. From the early Buddhist point of view this root is craving (*taṇhā*), a phenomenon which is, in theory at least, checkable not only for one's self but for others by anyone who, through meditation, masters a certain psychic power (*abhiññā*), enabling him to know the mind of another (telepathy, *cetopariyañāṇa*).

Since in early Buddhism it is a principle of nature, a principle of the way things are, that beings 'yearn for happiness and recoil from pain' (*dukkha*$_2$), it is appropriate to ask: where, if at all, does evaluation come into the picture? Is *dukkha* in any way an evaluative concept? The answer seems to be that in its more inclusive sense (*dukkha*$_1$) it is a characteristic of the *profane saṃsāra* in contrast to the 'no arising' and 'no falling' characteristics of the *sacred nibbāna* (with substrate).[10] For *dukkha* is so by virtue of impermanence, as pointed out at (a), and the cessation of *dukkha* and the destruction of defilements (*i.e.*, *nibbāna*) is not characterized by impermanence:[11]

> atthi bhikkhave tad âyatanaṃ, yattha n' eva paṭhavî na âpo na tejo na vâyo na âkâsânañcâyatanaṃ na viññāṇânañcâyatanaṃ na âkiñcaññâyatanaṃ na nevasaññânâsaññâyatanaṃ n' âyaṃ loko na paraloko ubho candimasûriyâ, tad amhaṃ bhikkhave n' eva âgatiṃ vadâmi na gatiṃ na ṭhitiṃ na cutiṃ na upapattiṃ appatiṭṭhaṃ appavattaṃ anârammaṇam eva taṃ, es' ev' anto dukkhassâ' ti....

> atthi bhikkhave ajâtaṃ abhûtaṃ akataṃ asaṃkhataṃ, no ce taṃ bhikkhave abhavissa ajâtaṃ abhûtaṃ akataṃ asaṅkhataṃ, na yidha jâtassa bhûtassa katassa saṅkhatassa nissaraṇaṃ paññāyetha. yasmâ ca kho bhikkhave atthi ajâtaṃ abhûtaṃ akataṃ asaṅkhataṃ tasmâ jâtassa bhûtassa katassa saṅkhatassa nissaraṇaṃ paññâyatî'ti.

F.L. Woodward translates these *Udāna* passages as:[12]

> Monks, there exists that condition wherein is neither earth nor water nor fire nor air: wherein is neither the sphere of infinite space nor of infinite consciousness nor of nothingness nor of neither-consciousness-nor unconsciousness; where there is neither this world nor a world beyond nor both together nor moon and sun. Thence, monks, I declare is no coming to birth; thither is no going (from life); therein is no duration; thence is no falling; there is no arising. It is not something fixed, it moves not on, it is not based on anything. That indeed is the end of Ill....
> Monks, there is a not-born, a not-become, a not-made, a not-compounded. Monks, if that unborn, not-become, not-made, not-compounded were not, there would be apparent no escape from this here that is born, become, made, compounded.

The second Pāli passage here (after the ellipses) shows well the contrast between the sacred and the profane in the early Buddhist context.[13] And it is interesting to note that in the preceding Pāli passage quoted just now 'the end of Ill' (*dukkha*$_1$) is characterized as neither arising nor falling, yet it is not characterized as 'something fixed' ('*thita*'), nor alternatively does it move. It is important to notice that *nibbāna* eludes conventional categories of experience and cannot, for example, be characterized as permanent by way of simple contrast with *saṃsāra* which is impermanent. This point also holds if one adopts the alternative translation of '*thita*' as 'eternal'. We have seen that 'everything impermanent is *dukkha*', but neither *anicca* (impermanence) nor *dukkha* as characteristics of *saṃsāra* enter into straightforward logical opposition with talk about *nibbāna*. It is not said about *nibbāna* that it is permanent, for example, but that duration does not apply. Although sometimes called 'the highest bliss' (*paramaṃ sukhaṃ*),[14] *nibbāna* is often characterized only by way of negation. Flew says that such terms as 'apostate' and 'infidel' have 'both normative and descriptive meanings'. '*Dukkha*' is a concept of this sort, having both a descriptive component and an evaluative component.

In the phrase 'he knows as it really is, that this is *dukkha*, *yathā bhūtaṃ*', 'as it really is', functions as an important qualifying phrase in that it brings home the descriptive-cum-evaluative aspect of the 'knowledge' of *dukkha*. There is an implicit contrast in any such talk of 'what is' with 'what seems to be', and in this context the implicit contrast is between the Buddhist (who knows *dukkha* as it really is) and the non-Buddhist (who does not understand *dukkha* in its more inclusive sense of *dukkha*$_1$). Thomas says: 'The ordinary man does not believe that existence is pain.'[15] Although 'pain' is not a suitable translation of *dukkha*, Thomas' quotation correctly emphasizes that the generalized ordinary view is that there are painful feelings of various sorts, but not that 'all is *dukkha*'$_1$.

'*Agha*' (as in '*aghamulaṃ*' or 'root of pain' at *Saṃyutta Nikāya* III, XXII, 31) means 'sin, error; evil, misery, distress, pain, adversity' according to Trenckner, who notes that '*agha*' is sometimes equivalent to '*dukkha*' and sometimes not.[16] And the Pāli Text Society's dictionary says of '*agha*': 'the primary meaning is *darkness*'.[17] Congruently it is also said that '*agha*' means 'the sky' considered as a dark empty void. *Dukkha*, however, does not have this latter meaning, and when the two terms are used synonymously this meaning of void or sky seems to drop out. For example, at *Saṃyutta Nikāya* vol. III, XXII, sec. 31 *agha* is used synonymously with *dukkha*, which had just occurred in sec. 13. In sec. 13 it is said that the five aggregates are *dukkha* and in sec. 31 that the five aggregates are *agha*. As Childers has noted, the terms mean the same here, and I suspect that both were purposely used in order to eliminate any loophole by means of which Buddhism might be incorrectly interpreted as having left open the possibility that in some sense or other suffering is not to be ascribed to the five aggregates.

We have noticed that *dukkha* can be physical or mental pain as well as a more inclusive sort of 'unease' (in the first noble truth). The Pāli Text Society Dictionary distinguishes fine gradations in the term's meaning, but no attempt has been made to investigate these here since the focus is on the first *ariyasacca*. But this much should be emphasized as noteworthy from this dictionary account on *sukha* and *dukkha*:[18]

> Sukha & dukkha are ease and dis-ease (but we use disease in another sense); or wealth and ilth from well & ill (but we have now lost ilth); or well-being and illness (but illness means something else in English). We are forced, therefore, in translation to use half synonyms, no one of which is exact. Dukkha is equally mental & physical. Pain is too predominately physical, sorrow too exclusively mental, but in some connections they have to be used in default of any more exact rendering. Discomfort, suffering, ill, and trouble can occasionally be used in certain circumstances. Misery, distress, agony, affliction and woe are never right. They are all much too strong and are only mental....'

Sukha and *dukkha* occur, for instance, in the set of the 'six elements':[19]

> Cha-y-imā, Ānanda, dhātuyo: Sukkhadhātu, dukkhadhātu, somanassadhātu, domanassadhātu, upekhādhātu, avijjādhātu. Imā kho, Ānanda, cha dhātuyo yato jānāti passati, ettāvatā pi kho, Ānanda, dhātukusalo bhikkhūti alaṁ vacanāyāti.

This is translated by Horner as:[20]

> There are six elements, Ananda: the element of happiness, the element of anguish, the element of gladness, the element of sorrowing, the element of equanimity, the element of ignorance. When, Ananda, he knows and sees these six elements, it is at this stage that it suffices to say, 'The monk is skilled in the elements'.

T.W. Rhys Davids and Stede, in making their above quoted comment that certain words are 'too strong' to render *dukkha* when it occurs in combination with *sukha*, have made a point which also applies to 'anguish' in Horner's translation. But another of their points, that 'agony' is 'only mental', is dubious.

Having examined the meaning of the term '*dukkha*' in the first noble truth, the logical status of the claim 'all is *dukkha*' may be investigated. The five aggregates mentioned previously as elements of personality are also, in conjunction with the respective faculties, constitutive of the universe. The *Sabbasutta* point this out:[21]

> Monks, I will teach you 'everything'. Listen to it. What, monks, is 'everything'? Eye and material form, ear and sound, nose and odor, tongue and taste, body and tangible objects, mind and mental objects. These are called 'everything'. Monks, he who would say: "I will reject this *everything* and proclaim another *everything*," he may certainly have a theory [of his own]. But when questioned, he would not be able to answer and would, moreover, be subject to vexation. Why? Because it would not be within the range of experience (avisaya).

Since on the early Buddhist view the five aggregates and the corresponding faculties are all *dukkha*$_1$, and since, as the *Sabbasutta* shows, the five aggregates and the respective faculties comprise the universe, it follows that 'all is *dukkha*$_1$'. From this claim it follows that all is *dukkha*$_2$, in the sense in which all compounded things are *dukkha* because impermanent. And from the preceding determination that *dukkha*$_1$ is a descriptive-cum-evaluation concept, it is clear that the claim 'all is *dukkha*$_1$' is partly an evaluative claim. This is a significant conclusion since it might be thought that the concept and the claim are entirely descriptive in view of the linkage between *dukkha*$_2$ and impermanence in the early Buddhist texts. This, however, would be to overlook the role of the concept of *dukkha*$_1$ in the evaluational contrast between the sacred and the profane. Few concepts are more fitting candidates to support Ninian Smart's claim that 'worldviews' have both 'descriptive claims' as well as 'existential force'.[22]

Pessimism may be expressed in proposition, statement, or insight about the world, or it may be a characteristic exhibited in attitude or temperament. *In actual cases both may be operative*, but nevertheless a distinction between cognitive and non-cognitive uses of 'pessimism' may be maintained.

According to Bryan Magee, however, Schopenhauer was not a pessimist, because he was not a pessimist in the second sense which I distinguished above. After making this distinction, one can see that Magee's argument is incomplete. For he ignores the sense in which pessimism is used cognitively and may be a statement based on observation of the world by giving an account of pessimism entirely in non-cognitive terms.[23] An example of his doing so is given after the discussion of pessimism below.

An inquiry into what is meant by 'pessimism' is necessary. It is important to distinguish between descriptive and evaluative senses of the term without, however, supposing that all usages of it must in practice fall into one or the other category. One consequence of making this distinction is that it becomes plain that it does not necessarily follow that because a view is shown to be pessimistic in a descriptive sense, it is *eo ispo* not a view of any value.

One attempt at a descriptive definition, neither honorific nor pejorative, is given by W.D. Niven along the lines that[24]

> In brief, Pessimism holds that existence itself is evil, that non-existence is preferable to existence, that the root of all evil is the desire for existence.

But this way of characterizing the matter is unfortunately open to two fatal objections. First of all in making 'pessimism' simply a matter of holding certain propositions rather than in part, at least, exhibiting a certain sort of attitude, many interesting *prima facie* cases of pessimism are ruled out. Individuals do not need to entertain general views of the sort which Niven puts forth in order to react to life in ways which make us justified in describing them as 'pessimistic'. Similarly Stewart Sutherland points out that atheism is not necessarily a matter of denying the proposition 'God exists', contrary to what some text-book definitions would have us believe, and that it may be expressed in much more subtle and interesting ways.[25]

Secondly, in tying the concept of pessimism to that of evil the variety of the phenomenon of pessimism, already restricted by a strictly propositional treatment, becomes further restricted in that many of those whom we would ordinarily describe as pessimists do not use theological-sounding talk about 'evil' at all. And in early Buddhism the world is not, nor is existence, evil—but it is '*dukkha*'. In early Buddhist mythology Māra, the personification of evil, tempts one to craving and grasping and hence to experience rebirth, and yet it is Māra who is evil rather than the world or existence ('profane' $\neq$ 'evil').

According to another definition 'pessimism' is a 'dissatisfaction with life' which is embodied in various philosophical formulations. It would, however, be too loose to speak of early Buddhism as being in this sense pessimistic. For the mature view of the Buddhist disciple after reaching the meditative stage of the fourth *jhāna* is not at all to be dissatisfied but, on the contrary, to have attained a state of equanimity incompatible with a grasping attitude of dissatisfaction. Thus experiences which usually cause dissatisfaction in worldly people do not disturb the mature, meditating Buddhist. It is of course necessary for one to become dissatisfied with ordinary life in order to be in a position to appreciate the attraction of the Buddhist path, but this 'dissatisfaction' is with *ordinary* life, not with life *per se* (both suicide and asceticism being condemned), and holds only in the lower stages of the path.

But the quotation from Niven allows one to make an important distinction, for reflecting on it one can see that pessimism as a set of statements is different from pessimism as an attitude.

Bryan Magee characterizes pessimism in the latter way by using an example which shows that in this sense there is no disagreement between pessimist and optimist about a matter of fact:[26]

> Two men who are drinking together shoot simultaneous glances at the bottle they are sharing, and one thinks to himself: 'Ah, good, it's still half full' while at the same moment the other thinks: 'Oh dear, it's half empty already.' The point is, of course, that they would have no argument about how much wine there is in the bottle, or about the accuracy of any measurement, photograph or drawing, and yet the

> same fact is being not only seen but responded to in two all-pervadingly different ways.

Magee says that although Schopenhauer is a pessimist, pessimism or non-pessimism are both compatible with Schopenhauer's thought:[27]

> And it is true that his pessimism is compatible with his philosophy—but that is only because the two are, of necessity, logically interconnected. Non-pessimism is equally compatible with his philosophy.

In the example and taxonomy which follows it becomes clear that this view of pessimism as non-cognitive is incomplete.

The story of Buddha observing an old man, sick man and dead man and subsequently formulating the first noble truth ('all is *dukkha*') shows that pessimism is *not* attributed to the Buddha as an *a priori* temperament. Instead he was depicted as a worldly prince who learned the place of suffering in the world by observation.

How may the cognitive strands of pessimism be expressed? Pessimism may be expressed as a belief rooted in (1) natural scientific, (2) social scientific, (3) historical, and (4) religious contexts. In (1) pessimism holds the physicalistic thesis that the universe or matter is so constructed that what is compounded comes apart, and hence lasting happiness (based on relations of parts) is impossible. In (2) pessimism takes the form of a philosophical anthropology which holds that man is by nature incapable of achieving lasting happiness or takes the form of a view of psyche which asserts man's being is replete with unresolvable tensions such that a relative adjustment to society but not lasting happiness, is the most that can be expected. In (3) pessimism asserts that an understanding of history shows lasting happiness to be impossible (for example because we are now in a dark age or because there will be an eternal recurrence of follies). In (4) pessimism asserts a view of the cosmos as containing more evil and suffering than good and happiness, and that this is in the nature of things.

(3) is a view found in Hinduism but not in Pāli Buddhism. The *Kali Yuga* or dark age is part and parcel of Hinduism but plays

no role in early Buddhism. (4) is a view held by Buddhists, but is based upon (1), since *dukkha* is analysed as arising due to *anicca* (impermanence). Thus, the Buddhist understanding of suffering is based on observation. This does not make it empirical, however, for metaphysical views may be based on observation (*e.g.*, yin/yang cosmology) but not be in principle falsifiable.

Version (2) is rejected by early Buddhism since it holds that *paramaṃ sukham* the highest bliss is attainable in enlightenment while alive. On the Buddhist view there is a positive belief in the perfectibility of mankind which makes it incompatible with pessimism in this sense.

In summary (1) and (4) express limitations which can be overcome, that (2) and (3) are not part of Buddhism, and the connection of these senses with the popular notion of pessimism makes it very misleading to call Buddhism pessimistic *simpliciter*.

In both its psychological form and its anthropological form (2) holds that there is something about man or about the psyche which makes lasting happiness impossible. Pessimism admits no consolation, as in Samuel Beckett's work. But Buddhism does admit of consolation. Our present lot is one's own fault and by effort, especially through meditation, one can improve it by a better rebirth (volitional consolation). Although it may take many life-times of effort, if one tries to reach *nibbāna* the amount of suffering will be finite (limitational consolation). Even in this present life one can limit the amount of suffering by the application of mindfulness (mentalistic consolation). Even when evil-doers (e.g., the finger-necklaced Aṅgulimāla of Buddhist legend) try to harm the Buddhist adept, no harm will come (the 'virtue is power' consolation). Recognizing that the world is full of suffering is the first of the eight steps on the Buddhist path, without which one is ignorant (the educational consolation). One can understand suffering as part of a cosmic scheme in which liberation is possible (holistic consolation). Since Buddhist thought sees so many sources of consolation, and since pessimism is a view in the absence of consolation, it follows that Buddhism cannot accurately be called pessimistic. Comparatively speaking, it is striking how many of the kinds of consolation considered by Boethius (some of which are mentioned above) can be found in the Buddhist context.

Consider this case:[28]

> The most thorough and uncompromising of the advocates of pessimism is Julius Friedrich August Bahnsen (d. 1881). He maintains that the world and life are not only essentially irrational and wretched, but will be eternally so; that his fellow pessimists have no right to promise that the agony of creation will ever terminate; that the hope of the extinction of evil in a world essentially evil is an unreasonable hope, and can be based only on blind faith...

Here although both the early Buddhist in the lower stages of training and Bahnsen have a 'dissatisfaction with life' and are in that sense both 'pessimistic', to say this and no more would be to conceal a great deal. For the early Buddhist would emphatically deny several points which fill out *in what ways* Bahnsen regards as unsatisfactory. It would be denied that the world is 'essentially irrational' and instead suggested that it is a causally-related sequence of events, the pattern of which is intelligible. And while unwilling to speak of the world as a 'creation' of *Issara* (Skt., *Īśvara*), the early Buddhists *are* willing to say that there is an end to man's agony, for liberation is possible given the requisite effort. Finally, the ray of hope that the system does offer for the cessation of *dukkha* is not based on 'blind faith' but rather on achieving some success through the practice of meditation.

What attention to cases such as these shows is that the attempt to link up various views as being 'pessimistic' may easily conceal important differences. For in filling out the reasons for, and reactions to, 'dissatisfaction', significant differences are to be found. As an analytical tool, therefore, 'pessimism' has precious little use. Nevertheless, prominent religionists and Buddhist scholars too numerous to mention apparently cannot restrain themselves from lapsing into vague mention of 'Buddhist pessimism', often without either clarifying the (descriptive) sense intended, or whether this is supposed to be (evaluatively) a bad thing, or how this term helps one understand Buddhism better.

Points like these should be clarified if the term is to have a limited use. Rather than ignoring allegations and descriptions of Buddhism as pessimistic, it is worthwhile to examine the appropriateness of this characterization. As we have seen, in the case of early Buddhism 'pessimism' in the sense of 'dissatisfaction with life' does not apply to the mature Buddhist but only to the novice. Even there not much of substance has been said, since 'dissatisfaction' may be found in radically different viewpoints. Secondly, even if early Buddhism were shown to be pessimistic in some descriptive sense, it does not follow *eo ispo* that it is inferior to 'non-pessimistic' views.

Western-educated people sometimes think of this world as a 'vale of tears' in contrast to heaven. As R.W. Hepburn points out:[29]

> The pessimist may see himself as in essentially alien hands, believing that he can conceive and long for a context for living—'elsewhere' in which properly human values would be realizable.

Since *parinibbāna* (*nirvāṇa* without the five aggregates after death) is not a state of being or place, the pessimistic view described by Hepburn is no part of the final goal of Buddhism. Hepburn himself sees the simple dualistic perspective of heaven and earth and its concomitant form of pessimism as erroneous:[30]

> To realize that there is this cooperative interdependence of man and his natural environment checks the extreme of pessimism by showing our earth-rootedness even in our aspirations. There is no wholly other paradise from which we are excluded; the only transcendence that can be real to us is an 'immanent' one.

In Buddhism the 'cooperative interdependence of man and his natural environment' is evident in many ways. In cave paintings at Sigiriya (Sri Lanka), and in numerous rock-cut sculptures at Anuradhapura and Polunaruva, man and environment are intimately related—not as viewers in a picture-gallery are with pictures. A *stūpa* (Pāli: *thūpa*) is circumambulated by Buddhist monks in a ritual round in a parallel (not identical) way to the way in which a pilgrim or an aesthete walks around a freestanding rock-cut South Asian sculpture. Aside from there being a world of cosmic symbolism embodied in the *stūpa*, the viewer-participant is drawn into a relationship with the stone structure. Thus the cooperative interdependence of man and nature develops through man's use of natural forms to depict, and moreover to participate in, the highest aspirations in the South Asian Buddhist context. How well Hepburn's quotation above fits this context! We are 'earth-rooted even in our aspirations...the only transcendence that can be real to us is an "immanent" one'.[31] There is no place that is named *nibbāna*, just as in Hepburn's Christianity heaven is not spatialized.

His argument is that on this distinction 'the pessimist may see himself as in essentially alien hands, believing that he can conceive and long for a context of living—'elsewhere', in which properly human values would be realizable'.[32] Although the Buddhists do envisage existing in *niraya* or the *devaloka*, the most common expectation is a continued earthly rebirth in some form. And there is a sense of the unity of life lacking in the 'value of tears' form of pessimism which Hepburn discusses.

In his well-known two-volume historical work, *Indian Philosophy*, Radhakrishnan says:[33] 'The aim of Buddhism is not philosophical explanation but scientific description.' If Radhakrishnan is right here, how do values enter into the picture? It is commonly accepted that science *qua* science deals with this 'is' not the 'ought'. Are we to say, then, that the statement 'all is *dukkha*$_1$' is on the same level as a statement like 'everything is composed of atoms'?

It might seem so, for 'all compounded things are unsatisfactory' is explained with reference to the scientifically-seeming claim that 'all is impermanent (*anicca*)'. But the doctrine of impermanence in early Buddhism is not a hypothesis put forward which might be falsified if counter-evidence comes to light. It is, rather, part of the framework in which concepts and theories must fit if they are to be intelligible in the early Buddhist context. Existence has three marks, one of which is impermanence, we are told; this is bedrock.

But how could the Buddhist respond to the claim that 'all is *dukkha*$_1$' is a confused one indiscriminately combining factual and evaluational elements? It might be argued that the very *concept* of *dukkha* is confused.

In reply one can present examples of concepts in other religious systems or in 'ordinary language' in which a similar combination of factual and evaluative elements obtains. In Christianity life is for instance sometimes described as a 'vale of tears', a conception which contains both elements. The implicit contrast with heaven indicates a description-cum-evaluation. As in early Buddhism the sacred and the profane are delineated, and it is obvious which is being evaluated more highly. In the case of 'ordinary language', however, the situation is more complex and it is not always clear from the words alone whether an evaluative twist is a positive or a negative one. To say of a man 'he is the king's *loyal* servant' is not just to make a descriptive point about a state of affairs, but is in some contexts to evaluate *positively* his being so. But saying this might make the man an object of derision in other contexts, calling forth a *negative* evaluation. But in either sort of case the concept of loyalty is partly evaluative, being frequently explained as 'doing one's duty'. The above examples function as a *reductio ad absurdum* against the view that '*dukkha*' is a conceptual confusion: if the concept of *dukkha* is confused because of combining fact and value, then so are many other useful concepts.

Overall it may be asked: has early Buddhism dealt well with the problem of suffering? Consider for a moment Job, who questions the suffering befallen him, blameless, and is answered:[34]

> Dost thou know the order of heaven, and canst thou set down the reason thereof on the earth?

and challenged:[35]

> Wilt thou make void my judgment: and condemn me, that thou mayst be justified?

but not intellectually satisfied, as Widengren observes:[36]

> The problem thus gets no theoretical solution, only a practical: man is commended resignation to the inscrutable will and majesty of God.

The early Buddhist position, on the other hand, has at least this much in its favor: it offers an *explanation* of suffering (but not a scientific one), how it arises and how it can be eliminated.

Immediately after Radhakrishnan's statement that Buddhism does not attempt 'philosophical explanation but scientific description' he continues:[37]

> So Buddha answers the question of the cause of any given state of a thing by describing to us the conditions of its coming about, even in the spirit of modern science.

But just because the Buddha gives a causal explanation it does not follow that he is *eo ipso* engaged in a scientific enterprise. The difficulty with Radhakrishnan's account here is that it falls heir to the erroneous notion that all causal explanation is scientific explanation.[38] Science explains by working with hypothesis and test and proceeds toward the construction of general theories. Like the Buddhist causal formulas, scientific hypotheses attempt to explain rather than simply to describe. But early Buddhism, unlike science, does not modify its views by taking into account the results of hypothesis and test. Nor does it offer hypothesis as a first step toward a theory which gives a rationally more comprehensive and better grounded explanation. Seeing the early Buddhist way is regarded as seeing '*yathā bhūtaṃ*', 'as it really is', and not in some provisional way.

Thus, 'all is $dukkha_1$' is not on the same level as 'everything is composed of atoms', say; neither is it a philosophical 'speculation' ('*diṭṭhi*') which is up for argument and counter-argument, 'wordy warfare' being condemned in early Buddhism. Here, as in many philosophical confusions, the problem consists in seeing too few alternatives: because early Buddhism is not a theistic religion that accepts the concept of God and the immortal soul, it is tempting to say that it must be either science or philosophy. But if we 'look and see' without this preconceived 'must' (as Wittgenstein for one urged), early Buddhism presents itself as a very interesting case which widens our conceptual horizons as to what counts as a religion.

To see the world with Buddhist eyes as a suffering world replete with ignorance and craving is at once to see the world as a theatre of conflict in which right view may win out over wrong view in case one manages to attain liberation. To see the world *yathā bhūtaṃ* is thus not to see what a video-camera would record, but is in part to see in a hopeful manner the possibility of liberation. To do so is to create meaning and value in life, in this case by transformation of the personality of five aggregates, with a view to liberation in the present or a future life.

My point here is that the creation of meaning and value is integral to the conception of seeing the world with Buddhist eyes. Once internalized this point sets a severe limit to the interpretation of Buddhism as allied to the spirit of impersonal Western science. The point is not, however, that the creation of meaning and value is unique to Buddhism. As Hepburn observes:[39]

> To say: 'Ultimately human existence in its cosmic setting is meaningless' is to utter only a veiled truth of logic. All meaning is created or 'projected'; and although nothing prevents us projecting it on to all sorts of human-scaled tasks and their achievement, it naturally cannot find positive work to do in relation to the remote regions of space and time, in which no human activity can make any difference.

'Meaning' is more adequately understood as an achievement or project when it occurs in phrases like 'the meaning of life' than it is as a 'raw given' that one 'finds'.

In this chapter exposition of the concept of dukkha has been given as it relates to the claim that Buddhism is pessimistic. My argument against this claim depends on an understanding of the nature and taxonomy of pessimism, and on the sources of consolation in Buddhism. These consolations do not include hope in another *world* of final peace, a view which itself works hand-in-hand with pessimism as regards this world. Buddhists offer an explanation of suffering more adequate than the one Job received and they create value in seeing a way out of suffering.

NOTES

1E. J. Thomas, *History of Buddhist Thought* (London: Routledge & Kegan Paul, 1971), p. 43.

2T. W. Rhys Davids, *Dialogues of the Buddha* (London: Pāli Text Society, 1977), vol. II. pt. I, fp. 255.

3I. B. Horner (trans.), *The Middle Length Sayings* (London: Pāli Text Society, 1967), vol. III, p. 329.

[4]Ibid., vol. III, p. 266.

[5]Robert Chalmers (ed.), *Majjhima Nikāya* (London: Pāli Text Society, 1960); vol. III, p. 249.

[6]Horner, *op cit.* vol. III, p. 296.

[7]Pāli *Text Society's Pali-English Dictionary* (London: Pāli Text Society, 1972), p. 325.

[8]Horner, *op. cit.* vol. III, p. 287.

[9]Rhys Davids, *op. cit.* vol. III pt. II, p. 97.

[10]Mircea Eliade, *Patterns in Comparative Religion* (London & New York, Sheed & Ward, 1958), p. 1 writes: 'All the definitions given up till now of the religious phenomenon have one thing in common: each has its own way of showing that the sacred and the religious life are the opposite of the profane and secular life.' It is clear that while *nibbāna* may be on this view considered under the rubric of the sacred, *parinibbāna* (by contrast) is not part of 'religious life' but is its limit, final extinction. I think one should take care not to apply the sacred/profane distinction indiscriminately, recognizing that the contrast between profane *saṁsāra* and sacred *nibbāna* does not hold in all senses of nibbāna. See Gombrich's criticism in *Precept and Practice*, pp. 155-156.

[11]Paul Steinthal (ed.), *Udāna* (London: Geoffrey Cumberlege for Pāli Text Society, 1948), pp. 80-81.

[12]F. L. Woodward (trans.), *The Minor Anthologies of the Pāli Canon* Vol. II, Sacred Books of the Buddhists Series, pp. 97-98.

[13]Eliade, *ibid.*

[14]MN I.508, p. 139.

[15]Thomas, *ibid.*

[16]V. Trenckner, *A Critical Pāli Dictionary* vol. I, p. 24.

[17]PTS Dictionary, p. 5.

[18]Ibid., p. 324.

[19]*Majjhima Nikāya*, vol. III, p. 62.

[20]Horner, *op. cit.*, vol. III, p. 106.

[21]D. J. Kalupahana, *Buddhist Philosophy* (Honolulu: University Press of Hawaii, 1976), p. 158.

[22]Ninian Smart, 'Religion, Philosophy & the Future' in *Encounter*, March, 1978, p. 54.

[23]Bryan Magee, *The Philosophy of Schopenhauer* (Oxford University Press, 1983), pp. 13-14.

[24]Hastings, *Encyclopedia of Religion and Ethics*, (Edinburgh: T&T Clark, 1913), vol. VI, p. 321.

[25]Stewart R. Sutherland, *Atheism and the Rejection of God* (Oxford, Blackwell, 1977), p. 5.

[26]Magee, op. cit., p. 14.

[27]Ibid, p. 13.

[28]The *New Schaff-Herozog Encyclopedia of Religious Knowledge* (New York & London, Funk & Wagnals Co., 1910), vol. 8, p. 475.

[29]R. W. Hepburn, 'Optimism, Finitude and the Meaning of Life' in *The Philosophical Frontiers of Christian Theology* (Cambridge University Press, 1982), p. 142.

[30]Ibid., p. 142.

[31]Ibid., p. 142.

[32]Ibid., p. 142.

[33]S. Radhakrishnan, *Indian Philosophy* (London, 1929), vol. I, p. 372.

[34]Job ch. XXXVII, v. 33.

[35]Job ch. XL, v. 3.

[36]C. J. Bleeker and G. Widengren (eds.), *Historia Religionum* (London: E. J. Brill, 1969), vol. I,fn. 309.

[37]Radhakrishnan, *op. cit.*, p. 372.

[38]To explain is to make clear or intelligible; to eliminate obscurity or difficulty. Since what counts as 'clear' or 'obscure' etc. depends in part on the sort of system (science, philosophy, religion), so it may be that what counts as an explanation or difficulty in one area is not so in another. More needs to be said about permeability of these 'systems' if they are not to be regarded as completely isolated from one another, but I have no time for that here.

[39]Hepburn, pp. 133-134.

CHAPTER 4

MIND AND REBIRTH

I

The argument of the first three chapters is essentially that the study of early Buddhism is neither methodologically (ch. 1), logically (ch. 2), nor emotively (ch. 3) flawed. These chapters argue for the rationality of early Buddhism and its study. In the next three chapters the turn is toward substantive points about mind in early Buddhism, viewed both emically and etically.

When mind is seen, as it often is in pre-twentieth century philosophy, as a 'something', it is ordinarily viewed either as entity or as process. In reacting against the Hinduistic substantive view of self as a kind of entity characterized for one thing as permanent, the early Buddhist view opts for the latter, process conception of mind. There is rebirth (*punabbhava*, lit. re-becoming), for which the three conditions of union, timing, and the presence of a *gandhabba* are essential,[1] but this is not to say that there is a permanent blissful center of consciousness (*attā*, Skt. *ātman*) which transmigrates. Much confusion may result from the failure to distinguish between 'rebirth' (as an early Buddhist concept) and 'transmigration' (as a Hindu concept), and I shall use these terms to mark the distinction. This is very important, for the idea of *ātman* is inconsistent with the first two of the three marks of existence,[2] is baseless from the point of view of Buddhist meditational experience, and, in short, plays no role in the world view of early Buddhism.

One misconception about early Buddhism is that it can (logically) make no sense if it is taken as saying what it really does say about rebirth. Since there can be no rebirth without a thing that is reborn, it is sometimes argued, rebirth (*punabbhava*) and no-soul (*Anattā*) are logically inconsistent. The assumption here is problematic, for there is a 'rebirth link' in early Buddhism, a topic explored in section II of this chapter.

To begin, consider the relationship between *viññāṇa* and *mano* as follows:[3]

> cha-y-ime āvuso viññāṇakāyā: cakkhuviññāṇaṁ sotaviññāṇaṁ ghānaviññāṇaṁ jivhāviññāṇaṁ kāyaviññāṇaṁ manoviññāṇaṁ.

This passage is rendered by Horner:[4]

> Your reverences there are six classes of consciousness: visual consciousness, auditory consciousness, olfactory consciousness, gustatory consciousness, bodily consciousness, mental consciousness.

Viññāṇa may be understood as 'discriminating awareness', and is subdivided as above. Here the relationship between *viññāṇa* and *mano* is one of genus to species: *Mano* is a type of *viññāṇa*, the part of a person's awareness which has to do with thinking. Elsewhere at *MN* I, 181 it is pointed out that the monk guards the *manindriyam*, the faculty of *mano* which, if not guarded, will ensnare him.

Since *manoviññāṇa* is a type of *viññāṇa*, and since it is clear from *MN* I.256 that *viññāṇa* is not a permanent thing independent of conditions for its existence, it follows that *manoviññāṇa* is not either. Of course this is not to deny continuity among a number of successives lives, for as the condemnation of speculation about one's lives in past, future, and present shows, and as K.N. Jayatilleke has pointed out, continuity was not denied. It is tempting to ask: continuity of what?—to which the early Buddhist reply is: continuity of the stream of consciousness. The continuity of life depends not only on the physical factors of union and season, but also on the presence of the *gandhabba*.

Concerning the *gandhabba* Mahathera D. Piyananda comments:[5]

> If *viññāṇa* is unavailable to the fertilized ovum, the ovum dies. The *viññāṇa* which is ready to enter the ovum is called *gandhabba* (Skt. *gantavya*), or one who is ready to go.

He further points out in a footnote that there are two usages of *gandhabba*, the one just given and another (derived from *gandharva*) which means 'celestial musician' or 'divine physician'.

But the claim that if *viññāṇa* is unavailable to the fertilized ovum, then the ovum dies, is objectionable on two counts. First, the Buddha is not depicted as making this claim, but rather differently as claiming that the presence of the *gandhabba* is one of the three conditions which are necessary for conception. Presumably, then, if there is a fertilized ovum, then the *gandhabba* was already present and thus the question of its unavailability does not arise. On textual grounds, therefore, Piyananda's interpretation here is unsound. Secondly, *ex hypothesi,* it is not clear why the being would die rather than be born mindless.

As for the condemnation of speculation concerning past, future, and present (rendering them in the Pāli order) just mentioned, it should not be supposed that knowledge of the past states is impossible. For at *MN* I.182 (trans. *MLS* I.228-9) it is noted that one characteristic mark or 'footprint' of the *tathāgata* is that 'he remembers diverse former habitations in all their modes and detail'.

It is interesting to note that knowledge of the future is not claimed here as a mark of the *tathāgata.* It is true that the Buddha is reported to have once made such a prediction, however, in the case of Devadatta—that he would be reborn in *niraya,* the low rebirth state of torment. The Devadatta case *might* be an interpolation, since it does not square with the usual avoidance of claiming knowledge of the future. This suggestion is obviously speculative, however, and taking 'early Buddhism' as a set of texts one may simply mark the inconsistency here.

As far as the relationship between *mano* and *viññāṇa* is concerned, there is also a distinction between the elements of mind (*manodhātu*) or ideas, and consciousness of ideas (*manoviññāṇa-dhātu*), *e.g.* at MN III. 62. In between these two *dhātus* is listed *dhammadhātu,* which is translated as 'the element of mental states' (MLS I. 105). Thus one has: 'the element of mind, the element of mental states, the element of mental consciousness', according to Horner. This translation leaves open the problem of how the second and third terms differ. Alternatively, I submit that the most straightforward translation of *dhammadhātu* makes the most sense here—'element of things'—so that one has: 'the element of mind, the element of things, the element of intellect'. Put a bit more broadly this means: subject, object, and cognitive consciousness as the relation between them. The relational term comes last, as in past, future, and present.

It is noteworthy that if one follows Horner's translation on this point, then mind, if different from mental states, would have to be some sort of organ or substance. Differently, too, at MN III.265-6 Horner translates *manaṁ manoviññāṇaṁ manoviññāṇa-viññātabbe dhamme*' or 'the mind, mental consciousness', translating '*dhamme*' as 'things', in line with the above suggestion.

There are passages which seem to support a view of mind as distinct from mental states, however. For example, it is said that the union of mind (*mano*), things (*dhamma*), and cognitive consciousness (*manoviññāṇa*) is contact: *tiṇṇaṁ saṅgati phasso* (MN I.112). Cognitive consciousness is seen not as a by-product of the union of the three, apparently presupposing that mind and mental consciousness are distinguishable.

Sometimes, too, *viññāṇa* is spoken of on one interpretation as if it is spatially locatable, *e.g.* at *Dīgha Nikāya* II. xv. 21-2, where it is said to 'descend' (*okkamati*) into the mother's womb. *The Pāli Text Society dictionary* has this to say about *okkamati*:[6]

> Lit. to enter, go down into, fall into. fig. to come on, to develop, to appear in (of a subjective state). It is strange that this important word has been so much misunderstood, for the English idiom is the same. We say 'he went to sleep', without meaning that he went anywhere. So we may twist it around and say that 'sleep overcame him', without meaning any struggle. The two phrases mean exactly the same—an internal change, or development, culminating in sleep.

Among the examples cited afterwards in *the PTS dictionary*, the very same phrase which Piyananda translates differently *viz.*, *viññāṇam na okkamissātha* (but taken from *D* II. 63), is rendered 'if consciousness were not to develop in the womb'. And in another place *the PTS dictionary* stresses the idea of entering rather than of developing, as in 'a god, on his rebirth, entered his new mother's womb (*kucchiṃ okkami*)' (*MN* III.119). Whether one stresses, on the one hand, the idea of *development* (or of 'entering' in the sense of developing, as in 'he went to sleep'), or, on the other hand, the idea of *descending* bringing with it the difficulty of spatializing the mental, one thing is clear. Continuity of a cycle of lives in early Buddhism does *not* imply the existence of a permanent substance as a substratum (such as *ātman* or *svabhāva*), which is supposed to be independent of causal conditions.

Does it make any sense to say that there can be continuity in early Buddhism without *ātmavāda*? The reply is that 'continuity' plays *different* roles in language and that the objection misleads one by assuming a single picture of what counts as continuity. As Wittgenstein points out in *Philosophical Investigations,* the strength of a cord does not always depend on there being a single strand which runs from end to end, but sometimes depends on the inter-relationship between overlapping and criss-crossing fibers, none of which runs the entire length of the cord. The early Buddhist doctrine of rebirth may be viewed like this: there is no permanent unchanging *ātman* linking up successive lives with *its* continuous psychic fiber, but there is nevertheless continuity which is assured by over-lapping and criss-crossing fibers. Buddhists sometimes use the metaphor of a flame in order to make this sort of point, since the flame is ever-changing yet continuous.

But what Pāli concept is applicable for the 'fibers'? And does this sort of view make sense philosophically? To take the first question first: the cognitive consciousness of a newly reborn individual depends for its development on dispositions (*viññāṇa* depends on *saṅkhārā*). As Kalupahana observes, 'when it is said that dispositions condition consciousness, it means that the dispositions (*saṅkhārā*, *hsing*), by conditioning consciousness, or more correctly the unconscious process, determine the nature of the psychic personality of the newly born individual'.[7] In this way *saṅkhārā* might be understood as the formative psychic strands of the rebirth process which condition the *viññāṇa* of the subsequent person. But in fact there is no one term which provides the rebirth link in early Buddhism, and it has been suggested that *citta* provides the link (Johannson), and that *gandhabba* does so (O. H. de A. Wijesekera).[8] *Viññāṇa* as a stream of consciousness might be taken as the link (Piyananda), *as long as one does not take it as identical and permanent* in past, future, and present in view of Buddha's rejection of 'this same one, not another... fares on' in the reply to Sati. *Mano,* however, never occurs in this connection. Thus, there are several candidates for the rebirth link (*saṅkhārā, citta, gandhabba, viññāṇa*), and no consistent, technical view about this matter in early Buddhism. But this should not obscure the fact that there is a clear view to the effect that whatever term is used, continuity and moral responsibility across lives is affirmed.

In the remainder of this section, support for the view just outlined will be mustered by criticizing alternative accounts, and later in section II the philosophical question just mentioned above will be dealt with in detail.

Piyananda writes[9]:

> According to the Upaniṣads, ātman is imperishable, eternal, has the shape of a manikin living in the heart, and is the perceiver, conceiver, and knower. In Buddhist thought, viññāṇa is passive, perishable, evanescent, formless, neither a perceiver, conceiver, nor a knower, and functions only as a passive force of the life-continuum, the major part of mind which continues throughout life and hereafter.

Piyananda also says that ātman is 'analogous to the Buddhist concept of *viññāṇa*', but that in the respects just mentioned above it is different. Of course he does not identify the Buddhist view with *ātmavāda,* but I think that the comparison might tempt one to adopt a mistaken picture. Comparisons are useful when they elucidate something, but it is not clear what could be elucidated by comparing the early Buddhist position with one it explicitly rejects.

Recall, for example, the *Mahātaṇhāsaṅkhayasutta.* Here the monk Sati is rebuked by Buddha for holding the erroneous view:[10]

> Tathā 'haṁ Bhagavatā dhammaṁ desitaṁ ājānāmi yathā tad-ev' idaṁ viññāṇaṁ sandhāvati saṁsarati, anaññan-ti.

Or:

> Insofar as I understand *dhamma* taught by the Lord it is that this consciousness itself runs on, fares on, not another.

The Pāli has the force of: the same one, not a different one. The identity ascribed to *viññāṇa* across lives by Sati is repudiated by Buddha, who emphasizes that consciousness is dependent on conditions and that if there are no conditions, then there is no consciousness.

Another passage which shows that on the early Buddhist view it is misleading to compare *viññāṇa* with *ātman* is *MN* I.139 (*MLS* I.178) where it is stated that whatever sort of consciousness (*viññāṇa*) is in question, all should be seen as it really is: not the 'self' (*attā*). Since the Buddha is thus reputed to have made it a special point to disallow thinking of *viññāṇa* as the self, a comparison of these two terms seems wrongheaded.

It should be noted that the early Buddhist position is not ambiguous about the notion of self. It is *not just* that there is *no evidence* for the existence of self considered as a permanent, unchanging substance or soul, but that there is nothing of the kind. For at *MN* I.136 (*MLS* I.175) it is said of *attā*: '*So evaṁ samanupassanto asati na paritassatti*' (or, 'he regarding thus that which does not exist, will not be anxious'). The term '*asati*' means 'that which does not exist', and so the meaning is very clear.

Denial of a self in the sense of soul which is always the same is not tantamount to denial of continuity, however, for continuity and sameness are obviously different concepts. The phrase 'continuity without identity' may be useful in this connection.

Suppose, for example, a string with different colors along different segments such that there is continuity but not identity, in the sense that although the string is continuous, its parts have different colors. Now in the case of the multi-colored string, one can ask the question 'what is it that continues?' and answer it with reference to the string. But can one ask the question in the early Buddhist context? If one does, this is like: 'what feeds on consciousness-sustenance?', the very question which the Buddha is depicted as rejecting.

Two attempts to answer 'what is it that continues?' in rebirth follow. Johannson, psychologist and Pāli scholar, thinks that *citta* 'includes all the layers of consciousness, even the unconscious: by it the continuity and identity are safeguarded'.[11] But he offers no textual support for this particular claim, and continues by citing passages to show that 'the whole gamut of Buddhist methods therefore aims at purifying the *citta*'. Doing so does not support the other claim, however. And as previously mentioned, Piyananda, on the other hand, employs *viññāṇa* as an *ātman*-surrogate.

If it is asked why there is no one technical term supplied for the rebirth link in early Buddhism, the answer can only be speculative. It might be that this is intentional, in order to avoid articulating a technical philosophical view which might be a source of attachment, or it might be due to diverse terminology being used by reporters of the Buddha's doctrine. But in any case it is clear that early Buddhism does not offer a substitute for the concept of *ātman,* as the passage declaring it nonexistent (*asat*) and the doctrine of impermanence (*anicca*) show.

As an historical note it is worth mentioning that a person (Skt. *pudgala,* Pāli *puggala*) theory developed in the *Sammitīya* wing of the *Abhidharma* school.[12] Proponents of *pudgalavāda* supported their doctrine that 'individuals (*puggalo*) exist as such in the truest sense' with reference to 'The Burden' (*Bhāra*) section in *Saṃyutta Nikāya* vol. III, XXII, 22, 1.[13] The crucial problem of interpretation concerns the lines:[14]

Bhārā have pañcakkhandhā
bhārahāro ca puggalo
bhārādānaṃ dukkham loke
bhāranikkhepanaṃ sukhaṃ 1

which are rendered by F.L. Woodword as:[15]

The burden is indeed the fivefold mass:
The seizer of the burden, man:
Taking it up is sorrow in this world:
The laying of it down is bliss.

In the second line Woodword translates *bhārahāro* as 'seizer', and mentions the interpretations of A.B. Keith and C.A.F. Rhys Davids in a footnote. Woodword insists (as against Warren) that the sense of *bhārahāro* is not that of *bearing* or carrying but of *seizing* or taking. I do not see that this move eliminates the *pudgalavādin* interpretation, for the *pudgalavādin* can still insist that a distinction between *pañcakkhandha* (the five aggregates) and *puggala* (the person) is recognized in the text.

Rather than focusing on *bhārahāro* as does Woodword in explicating the import of line two above, I think that more ground can be gained against the *pudgalavādin* interpretation by focusing on *puggalo*. *Puggala* means 'an individual as opposed to a group', and stressing this fact the sense becomes: each one carries the burden of the five aggregates *individually*, metaphorically 'bearing' this burden. To say this is not to suppose a permanent *ātman* under the description of *puggala,* nor is it to suppose an ontological distinction between *puggala* and *pañcakkhandha* any more than does *attā* as reflexive pronoun mean *ātman.*

It is evident that in early Buddhism, as in Zen, there is little or no theoretical interest in rebirth. *Punabbhava* (lit., 're-becoming') occurs several times, yet the focus of attention is much more on ending attachment and achieving liberation that it is on discussing rebirth. Perhaps it remained a 'conceptual grey area' in early Buddhism in order to avoid what is regarded as inconsequential speculation which takes attention from the Buddhist path. I do not think that the concept of rebirth in early Buddhism is muddled on the (mistaken) ground that an *ātman* or something like it in point of permanence is *logically* required. And some concepts do have 'blurry edges' and are nevertheless functional. Indeed, their usefulness *in the conceptual system as concepts* may require that their edges are blurry. Sometimes a slightly out of focus photograph could not be replaced with a sharper one and still achieve the desired effect. Thus, it is not a criticism of early Buddhism to say that there is no one term for the rebirth link (in contrast to what Frauwallner would have one believe).

There does not have to be some one term for the rebirth link as a precondition for its making sense. Kalupahana, although emphasizing the importance of *viññāṇa*, points out that 'this stream of consciousness (*viññāṇasota*) is the same as the stream of becoming (*bhavasota*) mentioned often in the early discourses'.[16] One may refer to the same process or thing by making use of different referring expressions, and thus the problem is not the lack of a single term being applied but rather the problem is the philosophical one of whether what is said with different expressions for the rebirth link makes sense.

There are two problems which can be raised here, the problem of the unity of consciousness, and that of the meaning of seeing things 'as they really are'. The problem of the unity of consciousness is really two problems. The first might be put: what keeps the personality separate from others while alive, what binds the aggregates?; the second, what insures continuity between lives?

In order to throw a little light on the first of the two subproblems, consider what the problem is not. Hume ends the treatment 'Of Personal Identity' in the *Treatise* admitting his inability, for the moment at least, to reconcile the two principles that all perceptions are distinct existences and that the mind never recognizes any necessary connections between them.[17] That this is not the early Buddhist problem, however, becomes clear when one sees that the position does not divide perceptions into 'distinct existences'. It is precisely this fact that makes possible an East-West philosophers' conference on Whitehead and Buddhism, since the process philosophy differs from Hume's on the point of 'distinct existences'. In early Buddhism there is no 'doctrine of moments' (*kṣaṇavāda*), as Kalupahana rightly emphasizes.[18]

Specifically, the conception of the *pañcakkhandha* (or five aggregates consisting of *rūpa, vedanā, saññā, saṅkhārā, viññāṇa*) does not commit early Buddhism to a Humean view of perceptions as discrete entities. It is true that *saññā* is often translated as 'perceptions', but it is at least equally justifiable to render it in the singular in the context of the *pañcakkhandha* as the PTS dictionary does: 'sense, consciousness, perception, being the third *khandha*'.[19]

In order to support this claim it is important to consider the meaning of *khandha*, which the PTS dictionary divides into a 'crude meaning' and an 'applied meaning'. The former is 'bulk, massiveness, (gross) substance', *e.g.*, in reference to an elephant's back, a person's shoulder or back, a tree trunk, and as a section of literature considered as a unit. It also denotes *e.g.*, fire, water, a heap of merit, or an abundance of wealth.[20]

As for the 'applied meaning', part of this refers to 'all that is comprised under a rubric 'in a collective sense' as either a mass, or/and very differently, as parts. Another part, however, specifically means 'constituent element' really 'in an individual sense', and it is here that Rhys Davids and Stede note that Buddhaghosa, the commentator, paraphrases *khandha* as *rāsi* or heap. Of course this gives it a particular slant: a heap is a heap *of* certain things, it is not a mass taken as a unit.

But Buddhaghosa's interpretation here need not be taken as definitive of the early position in view of the alternative possibility of construing *khandha* as 'mass'. Certainly there are passages in which the *khandhas* themselves are said to comprise a being in a way comparable to the way that a chariot's parts comprise the chariot, but this does not mean that each of them is in turn thought of as a collection of individual parts. Hence, the early Buddhist problem is not Hume's problem. Since there is no supposition that all perceptions are distinct existences, there is no problem of reconciling this with any other principle in early Buddhism. And if one asks 'what keeps the perceptions of a person together in early Buddhism?' this is to make the unwarranted assumption of the distinct existence of perceptions.

If one now returns to the problem of the unity of consciousness earlier posed, which soul-substance theoreticians may be inclined to stress, it can be argued that the so-called problem is irresolvable because it presupposes precisely what is inadmissible. For to ask: 'what keeps the aggregates of person A separate from those of person B in this life?' presupposes that something must, when it is not clear what that would be like. It presupposes that this unity is a problematic structure which requires an 'underpinning'. What would this underpinning be like? What precisely have we not got, that we might have? I submit that no philosophically defensible answer is forthcoming, because of the unclarity of what is being asked. As Strawson observes concerning 'the problem of the principle of unity, of identity, of the particular consciousness':[21]

> If there were such a principle, then each of us would have to apply it in order to decide whether any contemporary experience of his were his own or someone else's; and there is no sense in this suggestion.

The claim that there is a need for a mysterious sort of metaphysical rubber band to keep the five aggregates together may rest on a misunderstanding of the framework of early Buddhism. For an analysis in terms of the five aggregates is not the same as an explanatory account as to why things are one way rather than another. And unless one presupposes the need for such a logically odd sort of rubber band, it is not clear that a descriptive analysis is inadequate.

In one way, perhaps, the early position is more sophisticated than *Abhidhamma* attempts to systematize and 'rationalize' it, since it does not fall into the *pudgalavāda* error of thinking that a *pudgala* very like the *ātman* is logically required in order for rebirth to make sense. The *anattā* doctrine in early Buddhism is not a logical blunder, but it is an attempt to avoid a metaphysical one.

It remains to be seen what can be said of the second question posed, 'what insures continuity between lives?', in relation to philosophical issues of personal identity and reidentification.

II

In this section I shall first present some details of the non-substantiality (*anattā*) view and rebirth (*punabbhava*) in the early Buddhism of Pāli tradition. In doing so my intention is to present just enough of these details to be able to raise, in the second part of the paper, some questions of philosophical interest concerning rebirth.

If one wants to get clear as to what is being denied when the early Buddhist no-soul view is set forth, then it is important to understand the characteristics of the pre-Buddhist *ātman* view against which it reacts. As the Hindu view of *ātman* is presented, it is agent and controller. The PTS dictionary states:[22]

> It is described in the Upaniṣads as a small creature, in shape like a man, dwelling in ordinary times in the heart. It escapes from the body in sleep or trance; when it returns to the body life and motion reappear. It escapes from the body at death, then continues to carry on an everlasting life of its own.

This is a convenient summary of one strand of *ātman* belief, but as Malalasekera points out, while in the *Bṛhadāraṇyaka Upaniṣad* the *ātman* is regarded as unknowable, in the *Chāndogya Upaniṣad* it is regarded as not only knowable but as perceivable.[23] Thus one can distinguish two strands of Upaniṣadic talk about *ātman*, an agnostic mention and a more positive account. (Whether it is 'empirically' seen, as M. thinks is another matter.)

T.W. Rhys Davids observes that in the pre-Buddhist *Upaniṣads* the *ātman* has size, at first being characterized as about the size of a grain of barley or rice, and later as the size of the thumb (thus called 'the dwarf').[24] Rhys Davids reasons that since it is sometimes described as containing the elements of earth, water, fire and ether, it was regarded as material but with mental qualities attached.

Malalasekera distinguishes three senses of *attā*: one's own as opposed to others'; person as a mind/body complex; self as a metaphysical entity or soul.[25] Clearly the early Buddhist view does not deny the existence of *attā* in the second sense, as the five *khandha* (Skt. *skandha*) classification shows.

Applying the point that there are two strands of talk about *ātman* to Malalasekera's three categories, it is evident that his third category needs to be widened. He does not see that his earlier mentioned point about there being two versions of *ātman* belief (*Bṛhadāraṇyaka* vs. *Chāndogya*) needs to be applied to the triadic classification. Otherwise one gets an importantly misleading characterization of what the early Buddhist no-soul view rejects. It rejects the notion that there is a permanent mental entity called *ātman*, regardless of whether this is thought of as unknowable or as perceivable (through meditation). The texts stress that consciousness (*viññāṇa*) depends on conditions, so that when there are no conditions, then there is no consciousness.[26] Elsewhere it is said that there is no reason to be vexed about that which does not exist.[27] Briefly, we can say that the third sense of *attā*, the one that the no-soul view is directed against, is the sense in which *attā* denotes neither ownership nor observable person, but a theoretical entity whether conceived of as 'partly physical (*dehātmavāda*)' or as 'the life-breath (*praṇātmavāda*) animating the body, though different from it.'[28]

In early Buddhism it is thought that there are three characteristics or marks of existence: *anicca* (impermanence), *anattā* (non-substantiality), and *dukkha* (variously: mental or physical discomfort, unsatisfactoriness). The *anattā* doctrine has implications for the existence of any sort of metaphysical or physical substance. One might, for example, discuss the notion of *Issara* or Creator God in this context, but in what follows here I wish to focus the discussion on the no-soul view. And although early Buddhism disputes both that belief in soul is psychologically conducive to spiritual growth, and that there are adequate grounds for belief in the soul's existence, we are here concerned with the more philosophically interesting latter point.

Neither ordinary experience nor meditational experience, it is claimed, shows the existence of a permanent soul. Agency is thought of as one of the possible attributes of the soul, and at *MN* I. 231-233, there is a dialogue between Buddha and Aggivessana on this point. What emerges is that none of the five aggregates taken to constitute personality can be identified singly or conjointly as a soul or self, because like a king it would have control over what falls under its domain, yet there is no such controller of the five aggregates. Aggivessana is asked whether he has control over the five, whether, say, he can make his form change at will. It is in each case made plain that there is no such controller of the five aggregates. Perhaps Aggivessana suffers from the 'leading question' treatment so often dealt out by Socrates, for the argument seems to proceed with the implicit assumption that if there is an *ātman* who controls, then *ātman* must have 'complete' control—with no consideration to the possibility that a limited degree of control might be the most that *ātman* could muster.

Another *sutta* which takes a strong line against the idea of *ātman* is the *Sabbasutta* of the *Saṃyutta Nikāya*.[29] In delimiting what counts as 'everything' *viz*., the five senses plus the mind and the objects of each, no room is left for the existence of soul. How, then, is rebirth thought to occur?

The rebirth process (*punabbhava*, lit.: re-becoming) is said to occur according to a person's past actions (*kamma*). It is thought to be checkable that this is so by developing *abhiññā*, the psychic powers, and in some sense 'seeing' that it is so. The *rebirth* process is distinguished from the Hindu *transmigration*, and here I use these terms to mark the distinction between the sorts of view which hold that a *permanent soul* (*ātman*, whether construed as entirely non-physical, partly physical, or unknowable) transmigrates, and the view which holds that a stream of consciousness survives death in the case of an unliberated being and is reborn.

Prima facie there may seem to be a problem in reconciling the *anattā* or non-substantiality view with rebirth. It might be thought that a soul is logically required in order that moral responsibility across lives be intelligible in early Buddhism. If it is not the same soul substance across lives at T_1 and T_2, then in what way is one justified in regarding the consciousness at T_2 as that of the same person? And if it is not the same person, then what sense does it make to ascribe moral responsibility for actions performed by another?

As is sometimes the case in philosophy, the problem is with the question itself rather than with there being no answer. It would be a mistake to suggest, as the question does, that one needs to believe in the existence of soul in order to justifiably hold a person responsible for his actions. In a court of law, *e.g.*, it would be regarded as a peculiar and inadmissible argument to say that a thief is really not responsible for his crime done last year on the grounds that there is no soul substance making him the same person now as then. (If it could be shown that he was a schizophrenic, say, this would be determined on the basis of behavioral evidence and not on the outcome of debate about 'soul substance'.)

With this as background, some important philosophical questions can be raised: (i) Is rebirth an empirical hypothesis? (ii) Are there any criteria in early Buddhism for reidentifying a person across lives?

As Padmasiri De Silva notes in *Introduction to Buddhist Psychology*, there are three analogies used in early Buddhism to present the idea of continuity in the rebirth process.[30]

> The mind is a dynamic continuum which is described by the Buddha by means of a number of analogies. Sometimes, it is compared to a flame, whose existence depends upon a number of factors: i.e. the wick, oil, etc.—sometimes it is compared to a stream (sota), and again to the movements of a monkey jumping from branch to branch, letting go of one branch only after it clings to another, etc., are used.

Although it is questionable whether the idea of a 'continuum' adequately describes cyclic *saṃsāra*, a very important point is made in emphasizing the uninterrupted nature of the continuity, that *e.g.* on the monkey analogy, the monkey does not let go of one branch until he grasps another. As Kalupahana points out, there is no theory of *antarābhava* or intermediate existence in early Buddhism, this being a later development.[31]

Scholars disagree about whether there is a belief in disembodied consciousness in early Buddhism. Jayatilleke thinks that there is a notion of disembodied consciousness at work, as is evident in his taking *nāmarūpa* (lit., name-form) to be a psychophysical unity composed of sperm, ovum, and 'discarnate spirit' (*gandhabba*) or what is called the re-linking consciousness (*paṭisandhi-viññāṇa*).'[32] On the other hand Kalupahana regards it as 'quite incorrect to postulate a mind-made body existing after death, independent of the material body, until it gains a foothold on a new body in rebirth.'[33]

Although these are not the only twentieth-century writers to comment on this issue in early Buddhism, their difference here is representative of a divergence in interpretation. The relationship between each general view and each corresponding particular interpretation of a text is crucial.[34] For example, either *okkamati* is translated as 'develop' or as 'descend' in passages where it is said that rebirth does not occur unless *viññāṇa* develops in or descends into the womb. If 'descend' is favored, then it is accepted that early Buddhism has a notion of disembodied consciousness. And if 'develop' is favored, then no commitment to a disembodied consciousness view is made for early Buddhism.[35]

In the *sutta* where Sati is chided for holding that consciousness fares on, what is rejected is the idea that this *same* consciousness, not another, continues, suggesting that Sati mistook *viññāṇa* as *ātman*.[36] Thus it is not that the *sutta* rejects the continuance of a psychic element as such, but that it rejects *ātmavāda*. Consequently an appeal to this *sutta* will not eliminate the question of what the rebirth link is, as a basis for the ascription of moral responsibility. Whatever the words of the Buddha in fact were, and whatever his disciples and hearers thought he meant concerning rebirth, it is not an historical point but a logical one—and one which any account of early Buddhist thought must face—that the ascription of moral responsibility here requires the supposition of a rebirth link, regardless of whether an account of it is given in the texts.

There are three main sources of a reluctance to admit the supposition of a transfer of a psychic element in rebirth which can be traced to problems of textual interpretation. There may be others, but these seem to be the main ones; at this point considerations of the intelligibility of such talk are not presented. First, there is a misinterpretation of the dialogue with Sati, which arises by not noticing that the view rejected is that the *same* consciousness continues.[37] In effect this *sutta* is a rejection of soul theory and not of the possibility that *viññāṇa* might provide a rebirth link.

Secondly, there is an often-cited text which reports that the Buddha refused to answer the question as to whether the soul (and here the word used is *jīva*) is identical with the body or is different from the body, and this might seem evidence that he held no view of disembodied consciousness.[38] But because the point of his refusal may have been to show the irrelevance of 'wordy warfare' to the path, because the word *jīva* is used by the Jainas, and because no argument from silence can establish what the Buddha did or did not believe, the text yields no firm basis for the view that early Buddhism denied the disembodied consciousness view. And the continuity required in early Buddhism is neither that of the permanent *ātman*, nor that involving an intermediate state (*antarābhava*) wherein a psychic component exists without any physical basis. Thirdly, there is the apparent difficulty of accounting for contiguity as a characteristic of the causal relation if the supposition of disembodied consciousness is made. Kalupahana and Kōyu write:[39]

> According to early Buddhist philosophy life is a stream (*sota*), an unbroken (*abbhocchinna*) succession (*paṭipāṭi*) of aggregates (*khandha*). There cannot be any temporal or spatial break or pause in this life continuity (*bhāva-santati*), for the affirmation of it would be to deny the validity of the relations of contiguity (*samanantara-* and *anantara-paccaya*) of the doctrine of relations (*paccaya*) which is the corner-stone of Buddhist philosophy.
>
> The difficulty thus arising from the concept of *gandhabba* could be overcome and the problem of rebirth could be explained quite consistently with the philosophy of life as given above, only if *gandhabba* is taken to mean the death-consciousness (*cuticitta*) of the dying person. Then *gandhabba* would serve as the object of rebirth consciousness (*paṭisandhicitta*) so that the character of the newborn child would be determined or influenced by the consciousness of the dying person. Thus is the continuity of life set up without a break until the attainment of Parinibbāna.

About the reluctance to countenance disembodied consciousness as an early Buddhist view which this passage engenders, three points need to be made. First, there is no reference given here or elsewhere in Kalupahana's *Causality* to show that the Pāli terms for contiguity are used in early Buddhism.[40] In fact, one finds, both in this article and in the book just mentioned, that this is a *Sarvāstivādin* position. Hence there is no problem of reconciling it with the early Buddhist concept of *gandhabba.* Secondly, the idea of 'death-consciousness' (*cuticitta*) is also a *Sarvāstivādin* one, and is likewise a later addition. Thirdly, just how the 'character of the new-born child would be determined or influenced by the consciousness of the dying person' at all, but especially without the supposition of disembodied consciousness, is unclear.

So the sources of reluctance to admit the possibility of there being a view of disembodied consciousness in early Buddhism (different, however, from *ātman* in being impermanent) are not insurmountable. Some translations may mislead the casual reader into thinking that there is a single technical term for the rebirth link, for instance, 'the cord of rebirth'.[41] It would be easy to be misled by this into thinking that there is an early Buddhist term for 'cord' which designates the rebirth linking process. In all fairness it should be said that this translation does somewhat convey the sense of *bhavanetti* (lit., 'leading to becoming'). Yet there is no term in the text here which means 'cord', and without checking it might go unnoticed that the basis for the introduction of the word lies elsewhere in a commentary.

The problem of whether and how the reidentification of persons across lives can occur remains ((ii), p. 61). Are there any criteria for such reidentification?

Before addressing the question it is worthwhile to emphasize that a follower of the Buddhist path would not ordinarily be concerned with such theoretical niceties. Although early Buddhism does not appeal to faith as a justification for doctrines, the path-follower would say that such speculation on things unrelated to the elimination of craving (*taṇhā*), and the destruction of *rāga, dosa,* and *moha* or passion, hatred, and confusion, is counter-productive. The decision *not* to pursue certain questions is not tantamount to faith as a positive virtue in the way that Christians, *e.g.,* sometimes hold it, but the net result of staying 'within the fold', on the one hand, or 'on the path', on the other, is of the same sort. The anti-speculation of the Buddha is to a religious purpose, not to a positivistic philosophical one.

Padmasiri De Silva cites Strawson on reidentification in saying:[42]

> Attempts have been made to present logically adequate criteria for re-identifying persons in terms of consciousness, memory, and body. Strawson's position on this is very instructive: persons are distinct from material bodies, though this does not imply that they are therefore immaterial bodies. A person has states of consciousness as well as physical attributes and it is not merely to be identified with one or the other. This concept of the human person as a psychophysical being fits in well with the Buddhist analysis.

To an extent it does fit, since in the five aggregate schema of analyzing personality, one finds neither a physical reductionism of person to matter nor a view of disembodied consciousness *constituting* the person. Form, feeling, sensation, disposition, and consciousness are together said to constitute the person, and there is no talk of some of these being more basic in the sense of being able to exist without the other. So taken in isolation from talk about the rebirth process, it might seem obvious that there is no possibility of disembodied consciousness in early Buddhism. But the situation is not so simple, as was shown in discussing *okkamati* (descends or develops).

And it is not clear that Strawson's view provides any solution to the problem of reidentification of the person as far as early Buddhism is concerned, for he takes bodies as 'basic particulars' and observes:[43]

> These considerations taken together suggest that, if material bodies are basic from the point of view of referential identification, they must also be basic from the point of view of reidentification. That is to say, the reidentification criteria for material bodies should not be found to turn on the identities of other particulars except such as themselves are or have material bodies, whereas the re-identification

> criteria for particulars of other categories should be found to turn in part on the identity of material bodies. This expectation is amply fulfilled. If, for example, we take any familiar process-name, such as 'thaw' or 'battle', we shall find it impossible to give a detailed account of identifying a particular process of the kind concerned as *the same again*, which do not involve any reference to some material bodies or other....

A monk may claim to remember 'his divers former habitations' or those of others,[44] but whenever he compares a meditational image seen at T_1 to a body seen at T_2, or compares a meditational image seen at T_1 to a meditational image seen at T_2, or a body at T_1 to an image at T_2, Strawson's view of reidentification will not rescue the monk's claim to be seeing the same person. For on his view material bodies are basic from the points of view of both identification and reidentification, and in all three cases just mentioned the criteria fail to apply. In the first sort of case what is identified initially is not a body and hence it cannot be *re*-identified by an image. In the second sort of case a body is neither identified nor reidentified. And in the third sort of case no bodily reidentification takes place at T_2. Seeing a body at T_1 and a body at T_2 is not in question, for it is *meditational* vision rather than ordinary vision which is supposed operative. Therefore, since these cases are exhaustive, it follows that Strawson's criteria are not instructive, contrary to Padmasiri De Silva's suggestion, as supporting the monk's claim to be seeing the same person.

Strawson and Penelhum are both willing to give 'disembodied consciousness' just enough rope to try to show that there is nothing which can be hanged. Strawson does it by specifying the conditions (no perceptions of a body on one's own; no power to cause physical change) in such a way that the possibility of continuing self-awarencess of one's self as an individual hinges on thinking of one's self as a *former* person, so that one might have only a vicarious interest in human affairs. Consequently:[45]

> In proportion as the memories fade, and this vicarious living palls, to that degree his concept of himself as

> an individual becomes attenuated. At the limit of attenuation there is, *from the point of view of his survival as an individual,* no difference between the continuance of experience and its cessation.

This criticism, while perhaps a healthy antidote against 'spiritualist' views of the afterlife, does not touch rebirth or reincarnation, however, on which views the rarefied atmosphere of only thinking of oneself as a *former* person need not prevail.

Penelhum argues that although one can understand suggestions like 'Ruth is Bridey' in certain contexts, this amounts to nothing so far as the disembodied consciousness thesis is concerned, because: 'to say that Ruth is Bridey is not to say that Ruth-Bridey continues in between, and it gives that suggestion no sense of its own.'[46] Memory, he argues, is not an infallible criterion of personal identity, but one parasitic upon the body criterion. Thus, the notion of disembodied consciousness is considered unintelligible.

The force of Penelhum's conclusion that the notion of disembodied consciousness is unintelligible depends on the assumption that the body criterion is basic to reidentifying a person. In any dialogue with a Buddhist, though, this assumption would be question-begging, since it is fundamentally what is in question. Thus, the issue becomes one of whether or not the Buddhist can give any criteria for reidentifying a person which are feasible.

This problem is related to the problem about whether and how a rebirth link may be found in early Buddhism. O. H. de A. Wijesekera, for example, argues that *Amarakośa*'s gloss on *gandharva* (Pāli: *gandhabba*) as *antarābhava* (intermediate existence) gives an accurate understanding of the early *scholastic* interpretation, if not of the early Buddhist one.[47] *Amarakośa*, he argues, 'must have naturally been conversant with the traditional exegesis of the term, at least in the early Buddhist schools'. Yet as Kalupahana mentions, *antarābhava* ('intermediate existence') is not itself an early Buddhist term.

Steven Collins prefers to render *okkamati* as 'descends' rather than as 'develops', noticing that *gandhabba* is used in Buddhism to denote a type of 'spirit', at other times one of the three conditions for rebirth, and again as a synonym of 'birth'. In none of these contexts does Collins render *okkamati* as 'develops'.[48]

In this he is in agreement with Wijesekera, who writes of *viññāṇa* (taken as equivalent to *gandhabba*):[49]

> There is no doubt that it is used in the actual sense of 'descending, entering into'—the original (literal) sense as found several times in the early Nikayas in analogous contexts with the *accusative of that which* is entered (kucchim).

This interpretation of the nature and type of activity of *gandhabba* depends on whether one thinks that early Buddhism is committed to a form of dualism of mind and body or of spirit and matter. For if one takes *okkamati* as 'descends', then Buddhism is seen as countenancing the possibility of disembodied consciousness existing quite apart from the material world. It also depends on how one understands the relation between Vedic *gandharva* and Pāli *gandhabba*. For if one thinks of the Pāli term as simply borrowed without change in meaning, then the descending spirit view of *gandhabba* would be taken as comprising in full the meaning of *gandhabba*.

But there are good reasons why neither the disembodied consciousness view nor the *gandharva* view should be attributed to early Buddhism without reservation. First, as Kalupahana has pointed out, there is no theory of *antarābhava* in early Buddhism. Secondly, the Buddha refused to speculate on the relation between the soul and body in the famous ten questions set aside, thereby refusing to commit himself to a dualist picture. And O. H. de A. Wijesekera, in a detailed and convincing manner, has demonstrated that the early Buddhist use of *gandhabba* constitutes a distinctive development in Indian thought:[50]

> it would now appear that the term was deliberately employed by Early Buddhism, perhaps for the first time in the religious history of India, to denote the 'surviving factor' in man in contradistinction to the terms *ātman*, *vijñānātman* or *puruṣa* that, as seen above (§ 6-9, 16) were used to denote the 'survivor' in the Upanishads.

Wijesekera does not show that *gandhabba* is a technical term in early Buddhism, for as we have seen, *viññāṇa* and other terms can also be used to denote the 'rebirth link', an idea for which no single early Buddhist Pāli term is given in the texts. In his article, 'Vedic Gandharva and Pāli Gandhabba', Wijesekera does show, however, that *gandhabba* in early Buddhism is used in ways sufficiently different from related Upaniṣadic, Vedic, and Indo-Iranian terms to count as a distinctive development.[51] The mytho-poetic overtones of the antecedent term *gandharva* are so complex and varied that one cannot be sure beyond reasonable doubt just what were the connotations of *gandhabba* in early Buddhist usage. But one can be sure that the usage of *gandhabba* as one of the three conditions for rebirth along with union and timing constitutes a new idea in Indian thought. Consequently it would be mistaken to see the term as a poetic accretion in early Buddhism.

Rebirth does not logically require the notion of intermediate state (*antarābhava*) to make sense, but it does, at least, require the idea of a rebirth link. Since this rebirth link may be understood as an *impermanent,* a *changing* mental entity (unlike *ātman*), it is to that extent compatible with a belief in disembodied consciousness. It is compatible with this belief, but there is no theory about the matter in early Buddhism.

In focusing on Jayatilleke's phrase 'continuity without identity' some distinction between 'exact identity' and 'sameness' is required. For it is a necessary condition for ascribing moral responsibility across lives for an action x done by P_1 at T_1 to P_2 at T_2, that P_1 be the same person as P_2. P_1 may not be exactly identical to P_2 but must be the same person if moral responsibility is to be ascribed. Barring odd cases like multiple personality, P_1 and P_2 are clearly the same, and are judged so on criteria such as bodily continuity and memory. But if the task of reidentification is supposed to span various lives, then: (1) the bodily continuity criterion fails to apply; 2) memory, for all but an exceptional minority at the very least, does not even *seem* to indicate a history of previous lives.

But could there be, from a rather elitist epistemological stance, a view of the meditating adept who can verify previous lives of himself and others by making use of the reidentifying criterion of *memory*? My claim is that this stance is not consistent with the early Buddhist view of the world and time, so that if it were taken in fact, this would be a mistake. For there is a view of time and world on which these extend into an infinite cyclical past with no beginning. And unless there were a view to the effect that life came into being at a particular time, there would be an infinite regress of lives such that all the data would never be in as to whether the law of *kamma* ('action') applied in all cases and all the time. The 'law of *kamma*' (Skt: *karma*) might apply to some individuals and not to others; it might apply to a given individual through several lines but not very far back, and these possibilities cannot logically be excluded unless *all* the data are in. Since in an infinite series all the data are never in, the most the data *could* generate taken as empirical evidence would be a weakly quantified law and not the certainty of a world view about ethics and action. And the early Buddhist position does not present a weakly quantified law, but a view of what inevitably happens given the conditions (of craving or *taṇhā*).

One point that has emerged thus far is that Strawson's view of reidentification as requiring reference to body will not rescue the monk's meditation-based claim to be seeing the same person, *contra* Padmasiri De Silva. Thus in answering the question of whether early Buddhism provides any way of reidentification, it will not do to accept De Silva's view that Strawson's position on 'logically adequate criteria for reidentifying persons' is 'very instructive' for early Buddhism (p. 6). Care must be taken to distinguish the issue of what the person is from that of what criteria can reidentify the person, and De Silva does not do so in the passage quoted in which the appeal to Strawson's position is made.

Next I want to take up the question of whether the body criterion must be accepted for reidentification.

The issue of *conceivability* of an afterlife is separate from the issue of whether it is (in some sense, and this is problematic) *factually* in case that there is an afterlife. If one uses the term 'reincarnation' as a generic term to cover both Hindu transmigration and Buddhist rebirth, one can say that to believe in reincarnation is to take a stand on the second sort of issue. And about this sort of belief, it can be asked: what *criterion* (or criteria) can be used to reidentify a person in a different life? The following discussion attempts to show that the crucial issue is not this one but whether there are any necessary and sufficient *conditions* for ascription of 'the same person'.

A criterion is distinct from a condition. A criterion is the sign one uses or the evidence produced for making a determination. Unlike a criterion, a condition gives part (at least) of the meaning of a term, and the set of all necessary and sufficient conditions comprises the meaning of a term. What it means to be Lord Mayor of London, for example, requires a whole list of conditions, whereas a criterion would not give all that is required for meaning.

Memory, for example, might be thought to give a criterion for personal identity, but as a criterion it would not give the meaning of personal identity. In the section entitled 'Personal Identity' in the *Essay*, Locke maintains that memory is both a criterion and a condition. There are problems here, as Flew points out in 'Locke on Personal Identity', given this schema:

J_s	J_s	J_s
T_1	T_2	T_3

For if what it *means* to say that J_s at T_2 is the same as J_s at T_1 is that J_s at T_2 remembers himself as J_s at T_1, then meaning is dependent on the frailities of human memory. This obviously will not do, and needs to be reformulated as: J_s at T_2 is at least *in principle* capable of remembering. In the reformulation, however, one has only a *condition* for meaningful use of the term 'person'.*

Bernard Williams tries to rule this reformulation out of court. He argues that memory is a necessary, but not a sufficient, condition, since memory alone will not guarantee a way to identify persons in view of the possibility of two who claim to have the same memories. The most Williams has shown, however, is that granted a notion of personal identity *as we have it*, the body criterion is required for identification. But how different would things have to be for us such that this would not hold? Hick argues that there are cases in which we would not deny that x is the same person even if x disappeared and then reappeared. If this is right (and it seems to me so), then he has shown that the body criterion advocated by Strawson and by Williams *need not apply in all contexts*. It also follows that Penelhum's conclusion that it is necessarily the case that the body criterion is basic to reidentification when that turns out to be a contingent matter.

*I owe this point to Professor Stewart Sutherland.

Viewed as a condition for the meaningfulness of talk of 'the same person' across lives, it is also evident that memory will not do. It is absent from all but an extremely tiny minority of cases, except in cultures where there is widespread belief in some form of reincarnation. Even there the documented evidence is scanty. As a matter of empirical fact then, it is dubious that there are any such memories. Finally, even if one allows that evidence provided by researchers such as Ian Stevenson shows that there are some cases of veridical reports of past lives in Sri Lanka, such evidence is not incompatible with alternative explanations in terms of telepathy, nor does it show that reincarnation occurs in everyone's case. From a few isolated cases it does not follow that reincarnation generally occurs. In sum, it is doubtful that there are any such memories, and even if there are, their occurrence is not sufficiently widespread to supply a condition for the meaning of 'the same person' across lives as used by persons who neither have, nor know of any such memories.

But if one rejects the body criterion here in addition to memory as applicable to early Buddhism, is one left in a position similar to that of H.D. Lewis in *The Self and Immortality*? In a review of that work in *Mind* Stewart R. Sutherland notes:[52]

> One possibility which is considered and rejected is that of bodily continuity. In his discussion of this Lewis considers the case outlined by Bernard Williams, of two of our contemporaries, each claiming to be Guy Fawkes and to have the memories appropriate to being the continuing self who was Guy Fawkes. Lewis deals with this case by asserting that we should retain our belief that there can only be *one* continuing Guy Fawkes and that thus in the case of only one of the contenders can the 'alleged memories of a life as Guy Fawkes' be genuine (p. 103). Granted his rejection of this possibility and the fact that he does not believe memory to constitute, or to be a condition of there being, continuing identity, it is difficult to see what other alternative is offered, as an account of the nature of continuing personal identity.

It has already been argued here that memory will not supply a necessary condition in an account of necessary and sufficient conditions for the ascription of 'the same person' across lives in early Buddhism. What is in question is not whether there is a criterion, for marks or signs might be necessary and sufficient or might not. What is in question is whether one can have necessary and sufficient conditions for the ascription of sameness across life-times. And it is clear that the only other candidates besides memory, *viz.* self-awareness or bodily continuity, are irrelevant to the problem here. Hence it follows that what the early Buddhist position does or might consistently offer amounts to nought. Now I would like to suggest what might be said about this 'nought' from a philosophical point of view.

One way of distinguishing, in part, knowledge from opinion is to insist that a necessary condition of the former but not of the latter is that one must be prepared to give 'reasonable grounds' for the knowledge claim. This distinction is sometimes taken as following from an analysis of knowledge, according to which the three necessary and sufficient conditions are: 1) p is true, 2) X believes that p, and 3) X has reasonable grounds for the belief that p. If and only if these three conditions are met, some (notably Ayer) have argued, is there a legitimate claim to knowledge. Each of the three crucial notions in this account (*i.e.*, 'true', 'believes', 'reasonable grounds') may be subject to philosophical scrutiny, but I am not concerned about that here. Instead the intent is to call attention to the possibility that knowing something on this analysis may be not at all like the early Buddhist orientation to rebirth, particularly with respect to the third condition in the standard analysis. In doing so it is instructive to consider some of Wittgenstein's criticisms of G.E. Moore when the latter claimed to *know* certain things in 'A Defense of Common Sense'. The interesting point is that Moore has confused things which figure in the 'background' with things which can legitimately be regarded as knowledge claims, and hence it is clear that the term 'knowledge' is misapplied by Moore. (Wittgenstein has other criticisms of Moore, such as that his use of 'I know' is philosophically irrelevant, but I am not concerned to list them all here.) Speaking of Moore's truisms, Wittgenstein writes in *On Certainty*:[53]

> Everything that I have seen or heard gives me the conviction that no man has ever been far from the earth. Nothing in my picture of the world speaks in favour of the opposite.
>
> 94. But I did not get my picture of the world by satisfying myself of its correctness; nor do I have it because I am satisfied of its correctness. No: it is the inherited background against which I distinguish between true and false.
>
> 95. The proposition describing this world-picture might be part of a kind of mythology. And their role is like that of rules of a game; and the game can be learned purely practically, without learning any explicit rules.
>
> 96. It might be imagined that some propositions, of the form of empirical propositions, were hardened and functioned as channels for such empirical propositions as were not hardened but fluid; and that this relation altered with time, in that fluid propositions hardened, and hard ones become fluid.
>
> 97. The mythology may change back into a state of flux, the river-bed of thoughts may shift. But I distinguish between the movement of the waters on the river-bed and the shift of the bed itself; though there is not a sharp division of the one from the other.
>
> 98. But if someone were to say "So logic too is an empirical science" he would be wrong. Yet this is right: the same proposition may get treated at one time as something to test by experience, at another time as a rule for testing.

I want to suggest that rebirth may be viewed as part of the 'background' against which other beliefs in early Buddhism are seen as true by believers. In support of this it can be pointed out that 'there is rebirth' does not occur as a claim in any of the standard Buddhist schemas such as the four noble truths or the eight-fold noble path. (This is not to say that it never occurs as a reminder. One may be reminded that something is part of the background when someone expresses doubts.) Rather, the first claim of the four noble truths, 'there is *dukkha' presupposes* impermanence. This impermanence is understood to obtain both on the ordinarily observed level as well as on the not ordinarily observed level of the cycle of rebirth. Thus, the first noble truth presupposes rebirth as a part of the background in early Buddhism.

Belief in 'reincarnation' (used here as a generic term to include both transmigration and rebirth) as a belief in a cyclic flow of lives through different states is an abstraction broad enough to include both Buddhist and Hindu views of the afterlife. It is interesting to see how differently the Greeks thought of consequences of one's actions—that they followed one's children rather than one's self in a different life—but that here too there is a view of the human person's responsibility vastly different from the more individualist one in which there is no responsibility for ancestral errors or for a future of 'individuals' linked to the person one now is. What I am suggesting is that these beliefs need not be seen as a peculiar set of empirical propositions on the one hand, or analytic propositions on the other, in order to make sense. Alternatively they may be viewed as part of the 'background' against which other beliefs may fit or fail to fit, since the tests are devised *in terms of* the background. Treated as part of the background a brief is a *presupposition* rather than an *assumption* in an argument or a *rule* for calculating. To take one sort of example, the base ten arithmetical system is part of the background of many people, so that the system is presupposed in making and in checking calculations. Questions about the comparative usefulness of the system itself do not arise in making calculations in everyday situations, although students of theoretical mathematics might raise them. If they do, the base ten system is no longer treated as part of the background.

As section 96 quoted above suggests, a belief may be at one time treated as part of the background and at a later time be treated as an empirical proposition. Questions of truth or falsity do not arise insofar as a belief is treated as part of the background. The application of this insight for my treatment of rebirth is that 'there is rebirth' is, in early Buddhism, part of the background, but researchers like Ian Stevenson take it (he uses the word 'reincarnation') to be an empirical theory and try to test it by gathering data, (*e.g.* in *Twenty Cases Suggestive of Reincarnation*). On a strong notion of verifiability, however, which requires that the *in principle* possibility of falsification be allowed by specifying conditions for falsification, Stevenson's twenty cases do not show that early Buddhist rebirth is a verifiable theory.

To sum up briefly, the fact that what early Buddhism does or might consistently say about the problem of the meaning of 'the same person' across lives amounts to nought is understandable in terms of the texts treating 'there is rebirth' as part of the conceptual background of early Buddhism. This does not, however, make it a philosophically justifiable view. While treated internally as a background belief 'there is rebirth' does not stand in need of justification, viewed externally there is no good reason to accept 'there is rebirth', for it is not clear that the obstacle of providing conditions for the meaning of 'the same person' applied to a being reborn can be overcome. Neither memory, bodily continuity, nor self-awareness will work. Consequently, without some meaning-conditions, the issue of reidentification of the same person across lives cannot be meaningfully stated. For if we do not know whether and how conditions for the meaning of 'the same person' across lives can apply, then we do not have a meaningful basis upon which to seek criteria which might reidentify 'the same person' across lives.

Nevertheless, since the Buddhist empiricism thesis has been very influential in twentieth century Pāli scholarship, and since there is a claim in early Buddhism to 'know and see' rebirth, it is important to take up these matters in the subsequent chapter.

NOTES

[1]V. Trenckner (ed.), *Majjhima Nikāya* (London: Pāli Text Society, 1964) vol. I, p. 265; I. B. Horner (trans.), *Middle Length Sayings* (London: Pāli Text Society, 1967), vol. 1, p. 321.

[2]*I. e.*, *ātmavāda* is inconsistent with *anicca* (impermanence) and with *anattā* (non-substantiality).

[3]Trenckner, *op. cit.* MN I, p. 53.

[4]Horner, *op. cit.* MLS I, p. 67.

[5]Dickwela, Piyananda, 'The Concept of Mind in Early Buddhism' (unpublished Ph.D. dissertation, Catholic University of America, 1974), p. 91.

[6]T. W. Rhys Davids and William Stede, *The Pāli Text Society's Pāli-English Dictionary* (London, Routledge & Kegan Paul, 1972), p. 163.
[7]David J. Kalupahana, *Causality: The Central Philosophy of Buddhism* (Honolulu, 1975), p. 120.
[8]O. H. de A. Wijesekera, 'Vedic Gandharva and Pāli Gandhabba' in *University of Ceylon Review*, vol. III no. 1, 1945. Wijesekera argues that *gandhabba* has a 'doctrinal correspondence between its application and that of *viññaṇa*' on p. 93.
[9]Piyananda, *op. cit.*, p. 91.
[10]Trenckner, *op. cit.*, MN I, p. 256; Horner, *op. cit.* MLS I, p. 311.
[11]Rune E. A. Johannson, *The Psychology of Nirvāṇa* (London: Allen and Unwin, 1969), p. 30.
[12]Sir Charles Eliot, *Hinduism and Buddhism* (New York and London, 1954), vol. II, p. 101.
[13]*Ibid.*
[14]M. Leon Feer (ed.), *Saṃyutta Nikāya* (London: & Routledge Kegan Paul for Pāli Text Society, 1975), vol. III, p. 26.
[15]F. L. Woodward (trans.) and Mrs. Rhys Davids (ed.), *The Book of the Kindred Sayings* (London: Pāli Text Society, 1975) vol. III, p. 25.
[16]David J. Kalupahana, *Buddhist Philosophy* (Honolulu, 1976), p. 52.
[17]David Hume, *Treatise*, Appendix.
[18]Kalupahana, *ibid.*, p. 36.
[19]Rhys Davids and Stede, *op. cit.*, p. 670.
[20]*Ibid.*, pp. 232-233.
[21]P. F. Strawson, *Individuals* (London, 1959), p. 133.
[22]T. W. Rhys Davids and William Stede, *Pāli Text Society's Pāli-English Dictionary* (London, 1972), p. 22.
[23]G. P. Malalasekera, *Encylopedia of Buddhism* (Government Press, Ceylon, 1961), vol. I, p. 568.
[24]T. W. Rhys Davids, *Buddhist India* (Delhi, Motilal Banarsidass, 1971), pp. 251-252.
[25]Malalasekera *op. cit.* p. 567.
[26]V. Trenckner (ed.), *Majjhima Nikāya* (London: Pāli Text Society, 1964), vol. I, pp. 258-259.
[27]The word used is *asati.*
[28]K. N. Upadhyaya, *Early Buddhism and the Bhagavadgītā* (Delhi, Motilal Banarsidass, 1971), p. 81.
[29]David J. Kalupahana, *Buddhist Philosophy* (Honolulu: University Press of Hawaii, 1976, p. 158.
[30]Padmasiri De Silva, *Introduction to Buddhist Psychology* with foreword by John Hick (London, 1979), p. 83.
[31]Kalupahana, *op. cit.*, p. 52.
[32]K. N. Jayatilleke, *The Message of the Buddha* edited by Ninian Smart (London, 1975), p. 82.
[33]D. J. Kalupahana and Kōyu Tamura, 'Antarābhava' in G.P. Malalasekera, *op. cit.*, p. 731.
[34]Rhys Davids & Stede *op. cit.*, p. 163; see also *e.g.*, *Dīgha Nikāya* II, p. 63.

[35]Steven Collins has elaborated the interpretation of *okkamati* as 'descends' in his work, *Selfless Persons* (Cambridge University Press, 1982), pp. 208-213.

[36]De Silva *op. cit.*, pp. 83-84.

[37]*Ibid.*, p. 258.

[38]Trenckner, *op. cit.*, p. 426.

[39]Kalupahana and Kōyu, *op. cit.*, p. 731.

[40]David J. Kalupahana, *Causality: The Central Philosophy of Buddhism* (Honolulu: University Press of Hawaii, 1975), pp. 60-61.

[41]L. Feer (ed.), and Mrs. C.A.F. Rhys Davids with F.L. Woodward (trans.), *The Book of the Kindred Sayings* vol. III, p. 157.

[42]De Silva, *op. cit.*, pp. 83-84.

[43]P. F. Strawson, *Individuals* (London, 1959), p. 55.

[44]This is a frequently recurring phrase in the Canon. See Kalupahana, *Buddhist Philosophy* pp. 21-22 for a schema of *abhiññā*.

[45]Strawson, *op. cit.*, p. 116.

[46]Terence Penelhum, *Survival and Disembodied Consciousness* (London: 1970), p. 91.

[47]O. H. de A. Wijesekera, 'Vedic Gandharva and Pāli Gandhabba' in *University of Ceylon Review* vol. III, no. 1, p. 89.

[48]Collins, *op. cit.*, pp. 210-213.

[49]O. H. de A. Wijesekera, 'Vedic Gandharva and Pāli Gandhabba' in *University of Ceylon Review* 1945, vol. III, no. 1, p. 92.

[50]*Ibid.*, p. 95.

[51]*Ibid.*, *passim.* Wijesekera traces the development of Iranian *gandarewa*, Vedic *gandharva*, and Pāli *gandhabba* in a masterly and detailed manner which eludes capsule summary. Among the numerous associations of *gandharva* are those with water and sexuality, and these are especially appropriate to understanding the background of early Buddhist *gandhabba*.

[52]Stewart R. Sutherland, review of H.D. Lewis, *The Self and Immortality* (London, Macmillan, 1973) in *Mind* vol. LXXXV no. 337, January 1976, p. 143. I am indebted to Sutherland for several comments about criteria and conditions.

[53]Ludwig Wittgenstein, *On Certainty* edited by G.E.M. Anscombe and G.H. von Wright (Oxford, Basil Blackwell, 1977), p. 15e.

CHAPTER 5

MIND AND VERIFICATION

The structure of this chapter is, in section I to discuss the roles of *saddhā* ('confidence', 'faith'), in II *abhiññā* ('higher kinds of knowledge and psychic powers') and evidence, and in III the Buddhist empiricism thesis. It is informed by the conviction that the understanding of these topics is interrelated, and that this sequence facilitates understanding better than, say, reversing sections I and II would. For if one begins with a view of early Buddhism as epistemological philosophy, then certain uses of *saddhā* may be ignored as anomalous data which do not fit the preconceived view. In section III the view that *abhiññā* can be interpreted as the epistemological basis of early Buddhism is examined and rejected on both internal textual and external philosophical grounds. As a result, some features of religious belief emerge sharply.

I

In discussing the roles of *saddhā* the issues of the relation between confidence and learning the doctrine, between confidence and practical results, and the interpretation of *amūlikā saddhā* and *ākāravatī saddhā* are crucial.[1]

To begin with the relation between confidence and learning the doctrine, consider two passages from the *Majjhima Nikāya*:[2]

> When I had heard that *dhamma* I gained faith in the *Tathāgata*

and:[3]

> If faith is born, then he approaches.

The first might be viewed (mistakenly) as support for the notion that *saddhā* is only consequent to checking. Not only is it confidence in the *Tathāgata* (rather than in the doctrine specifically) which results, but this quotation is balanced by others like the second in which *saddhā* is prior to investigation. From an epistemological perspective, therefore, *saddhā* sometimes precedes and is not always consequent to checking the doctrine.

It is also illuminating to see *saddhā* from a pragmatic perspective, in terms of whether it follows or precedes practical realization on the path. On the one hand, considering learning elephant riding and handling the goad (which are compared with becoming a Buddhist adept) it is said (MN II 94, MLS II 281):

> Had he no faith he could not attain whatever is to be won by faith.

In this context *saddhā* is one of the five qualities (*pañca vasāṇi*) for making progress on the path, and is *prior* to achieving results. In the same vein is the *Saṃyutta Nikāya* passage where development of *abhiññā* depends on *saddhā*.[4]

On the other hand, *saddhā* comes after getting results, after hearing the doctrine. 'Be a *dīpa* (lamp, island) for yourself,' the trainee is urged, and do not accept anything on report, tradition, or hearsay, but because you have known and seen it yourself.[5]

Saddhā is one of the five powers which taken together define the *Arahant* when they are fully developed. Having a proper degree of faith, energy, mindfulness, concentration and insight is to have the necessary and sufficient conditions for becoming an *Arahant*[6]. But in addition to this sort of usage of *saddhā* as an *indriya* (faculty) as in the phrase 'the moral sense of faith', it also occurs in expressions like 'walking according to faith' and 'living in faith'.[7]

A very different usage is exemplified in the story of the wanderer, Magandiya, proud of his health, who is told by the Buddha that such pride is like being taken in by a confidence man. Being proud of one's health is compared to 'confidence in the man with vision' (*i.e.*, the trickster) who offers a greasy, grimy, coarse robe as if it were a lovely, unstained, pure, white cloth.[8] The word used is *saddhā*, and thus one finds that *saddhā* is not always regarded as a good thing.

Elsewhere in the *Majjhima Nikāya*, however, there is a clear contrast between: 'a good man has faith' and 'a bad man is lacking in faith'.[9] *Saddhā* is here used with a pro-attitude, as in the five qualities usage. There are degrees of *saddhā*, as the difference between those 'with only a little faith, with only a little regard' and those 'who have gone forth from home into homelessness without faith, who are crafty' shows.[10] The latter is contrasted with the phrase, those who have 'gone forth from home into homelessness through faith in me'.[11] When *saddhā* is used as a virtue it is linked to moral habits involving certain attitudes as in the 'young men of family who have faith and are of great enthusiasm, of great joyousness and who, having heard this, focus their minds on suchness.'[12] That moral habit is seen as an important way of developing *saddhā* as a virtue is clear in the emphasis given to family background, 'he who comes from a family that has no faith' being at an initial, though not necessarily final, disadvantage.[13]

The 'object' or focus of *saddhā* may be the Buddha, the doctrine, or the Order of monks. Sometimes these are mentioned singly, and sometimes in combination, although there is no one of them which is always present in descriptions of the object of faith.[14]

There is no evidence of a division among the uses of *saddhā* such that confidence in the doctrine is a primary use and the others of lesser importance. For there are affective rather than cognitive uses like 'if faith is born, then he approaches' in order to hear the doctrine. Although it would be a mistake to over-emphasize a single strand of the complex concept as more important than all others, there are some passages which suggest the over-riding importance of *saddhā* in the *Tathāgata*, for example:[15]

> If he has enough faith in the Tathāgata, enough regard, then he will have these things, that is to say the faculty of faith, the faculty of energy, the faculty of mindfulness, the faculty of concentration, the faculty of wisdom. This, monk, is called the person who is striving after faith.

If it is correct to assume that the second occurrence of *saddhā* here, as in 'the faculty of faith', refers to doctrine, then one *consequence* of sufficient faith in the *Tathāgata* is faith in the doctrine. Taken in this way, the passage depicts the former as the source or precondition of the latter. I mention this passage not to argue for one usage of *saddhā* as primary in general, but to offset the undue weight given to *ākāravatī saddhā* (Jayatilleke: 'rational faith').[16]

Jayatilleke calls attention to a distinction presented in the *Majjhima Nikāya* between confidence based on checking some points of the doctrine by acquiring 'knowledge and vision' (which is called 'rational faith', MN I 320), and the 'baseless faith' (*amūlikā saddhā*) which the brahmins are said to have had toward the Vedas. Now it is important that he calls attention to this distinction, and although he shows awareness that there are many strands to the concept of *saddhā*, yet in his attempt to give an account of the concept, a reductionistic account in terms of propositional belief emerges according to which all uses telescope into the cognitive strand.[17]

> (659) The object of saddhā in the Nikāyas is most frequently the Buddha. The favourite phrase is 'having heard his doctrine he acquired faith in the Tathāgata' (taṃ dhammaṃ sutvā Tathāgate saddhāṃ paṭilabhati, M.I. 179, 267, 344; M. III. 33). If saddhā means 'belief, 'acquiring faith in the Buddha' is equivalent to saying 'believing in the Buddha' and what is meant by believing in the Buddha is that one believes that what the Buddha says is true. As Woozley points out, 'certainly we do talk of believing in a person but there we mean that we believe that what he says is true.' The verb, pasīdati, 'to have faith in, appreciate' also has the person of the Buddha as the object (*e.g.* Satthari pasīdiṃ, M.I. 320) but pasāda—in the compound aveccappasāda—(v. supra, 655) frequently has the Buddha, his teaching (Dhamma) and his Order (Saṅgha) as the objects. Here 'faith' or belief in the Dhamma means the statements that constitute the Dhamma or the teachings of the Buddha. Likewise, believing in the Saṅgha implies believing in the truth of the utterances of the Saṅgha; since these were more or less derived from the Buddha, it again ultimately implies a belief in the statements of the Buddha.

The third sentence above in particular states that believing in the Buddha and believing that what the Buddha says is true are *equivalent*. What Jayatilleke is doing here is giving an account of *saddhā* such that all its uses are parasitical upon its cognitive use. There are two major difficulties with this attempt. First, it is mistaken to suppose (with Woozley) that believing in a person is tantamount to believing that what he says is true. For as Mitchell's parable of the Stranger shows, belief in a person sometimes occurs even where it is recognized that the person says things that are false. Secondly, even if this supposition of equivalence were philosophically defensible, it would not be factually correct to think that in early Buddhism the cognitive sense of *saddhā* is primary or fundamental. For prior to knowing the doctrine *saddhā* is sometimes important, as in 'if faith is born, then he approaches' and 'had he no faith he could not attain whatever is to be won by faith'. There is thus an affective element in *saddhā* which is ignored if one treats believing in the Buddha as equivalent to believing that what he says is true.

Unfortunately Jayatilleke's attendance at some of Wittgenstein's lectures does not help him to avoid the 'craving for generality' that underlies his search for a basic, general meaning of *saddhā* as cognitive. Seeing the futility of this search has implications for the Buddhist empiricism thesis to be discussed in III, and facilitates a clearer view of the next topic, *abhiññā* and evidence, in II.*

II

In 'St. Paul's Damascus Experience' Stewart Sutherland argues against interpreting unusual experiences as *evidence* for religious belief. He argues for the view that:[18]

> Initially and fundamentally a religious experience is characterized as such in the light of the role which it plays in the life of the individual in question, rather than in the light of any unusual perceptions, or celestial fireworks display which may accompany that experience.

*Elsewhere, from a similar starting point to that in section I above, I have discussed some philosophical implications of an understanding of *saddhā* in early Buddhism for the problem of the relation between faith and the justification of religious belief. An abstract of the paper presented may be found in *Interpreting Across Boundaries*, proceedings of the International Research Conference for Asian and Comparative Philosophy, August 13-17, 1984, Honolulu. The paper is to be published in *Journal of Indian Philosophy* 15 (1987), pp. 97-110.

The conclusion results from a consideration of two possibilities regarding religious experience, and in particular, St. Paul's Damascus road experience, as to whether or not there being divergent accounts of such an experience matters for understanding religious belief. A skeletal paraphrase of the argument is that, where p means 'God spoke to Paul', there are three possibilities: p is denied, p is taken as equivocally true, and p is taken as univocally true. All of these responses take it as obvious that divergent accounts of the experience matter, but Sutherland argues that certain common features of these responses imply:[19]

> a view of faith in which the role given to religious experience is that of justifying or providing grounds for belief. The authenticity or credibility of faith then rests upon the validity of the claim to have had authoritative or credible religious experience.

And this, the argument continues, results in a cleavage between religious life and belief on the one hand, and a somehow isolated religious experience on the other. Thus, since the hypothesis that divergent accounts of religious experience matter for understanding religious belief has led to this absurdity, Sutherland examines the alternative concerning St. Paul, favouring the view 'that the discrepancies in the three accounts of St. Paul's experience are not significant.'[20]

Sutherland's movement from a Christo-centric consideration of religious experience on the road to Damascus to 'general conclusions' about 'our understanding of the nature of religious experience' may be questioned by those who are not convinced by the force of a single example, however central that example may be to Christianity.[21] In what follows I propose to examine religious experience under the *bodhi* tree on the bank of the river Nerañjarā in order to see if corroboration of the general conclusion is available in Buddhism.

As far as 'celestial fireworks' and the like are concerned the Buddha is depicted as warning against using magical tricks in order to gain converts. And, as Jayatilleke cleverly puts it,[22]

> he speaks of the dangers of performing wonders and of thought reading in public, while speaking in praise of

> 'the miracle of instruction' (*anusāsanipāṭihāriyam*, D. I. 214), which in fact was instruction without a miracle.

Further, that enlightenment in early Buddhism is not just a momentary psychological state of a trivial sort, but one which is explained by reference to beliefs, is evident from the *Udāna* passage allegedly uttered just after Buddha's enlightenment:[23]

> When, indeed, things appear
> To the brahman in deep reflection,
> All his doubts disappear
> As he understands their causal nature.

Two points of agreement between the Damascus road and the Nerañjarā river experiences emerge: first, the experiences are not just titillations of individual awareness in a dramatic way, but involve a change in beliefs. Secondly, this change in beliefs is marked by actions which show conviction that the path is right.

The first point, change in beliefs, might be considered the religious analogue to paradigm shift in science. Basil Mitchell remarks:[24]

> When a choice has to be made between high-level scientific theories or paradigms, the choice cannot be determined wholly by observation or by strict rules of logic; for both the rival paradigms are logically in order and both have access to the same observations and can give an account of them.

Historically viewed early Buddhism emerges out of a context in which the Buddha had utilized Hindu meditation techniques common at that time. Yet it is also said that the Buddha did not rest content with the teachings of his mentors, Alāra Kālāma and Uddaka Rāmaputta.[25] As an important addition to their views he added the sixth *abhiññā*: knowledge of the destruction of defilements (*āsavas*) which keep one within the cycle of birth and death.

Of the Hindu sages who meditated, some claimed that the *ātman* is perceivable. While one strand of Upaniṣadic talk about *ātman* regards it as perceivable, another regards it as unknowable. It is a curious fact that in the early dialogues Buddha never encounters anyone who actually claims to have seen the *ātman*. It is speculative as to whether this is due more to careful editing by the Buddhists who compiled the Pāli Canon or to the availability of a meditator willing to make such a bold claim. There is a *conceptual* difficulty with what an experience would be like so as to guarantee that the attribute of permanence applies to a soul substance allegedly known through introspection. And according to the Buddhist paradigm it is clear that there is no room for *ātman*.

It is well-known that the Buddha rejected both the eternalist and annihilationist views. The rejection of the former is a rejection of *ātmavāda*, soul theory, in any formulation—particularly the concept of a permanent thing which it involves. This does not of course rule out the stream of consciousness view of rebirth, for the stream is, like everything else in the world, viewed as impermanent. The rejection of annihilationism is, I submit, a rejection of *Cārvāka* ('materialism') in its denial of *kamma* (action) having an effect in another life (whether understood in Hindu or in Buddhist terms of continuity). If my suggestion is correct, then it is a mistake to think that the Buddha's rejection of annihilationism is a rejection of the idea that 'final enlightenment' (*parinibbāna*) is extinction. But this way of putting the matter leaves open the problem of interpreting 'the deathless' (*amata*) as an attribute of enlightenment, a problem which I shall take up in Ch. 6.

As there are different points of view from which Buddhism may be described, there are accordingly different doctrines which may appear as central. I do not want to make any claim about what the 'central philosophy' of Buddhism is, but to say that to take two examples, causality and rebirth, either can show that the early Buddhist position is different from preexisting tradition. Clearly the early Buddhist view of rebirth is distinctive. E. J. Thomas, however, comes all too close to stating that the Buddha says only what the Hindus had been saying all along about rebirth and *karma*, when he claims that Buddhism 'inherited' these views.[26] At a sufficiently lofty level of generality, of course, one might claim that Buddhist and Hindu views are 'the same' in holding that 'we will live on, unless liberated', but this move is useless for understanding the distinctive contributions of each.

I would like now to return and develop the second point of agreement between Damascus road and Nerañjarā bank, that is, that the change in beliefs precedes a change of life. On Sutherland's view of the Damascus road experience:[27]

> to understand the significance of that experience—what makes it religious—is to grasp the role which it plays in the life of the believer. The experience modifies how he sees his life, how he behaves, and so on, and in parallel fashion the way in which he sees the experience in question may alter in the light of his developing biography. The attempt to understand a particular experience in the absence of at least some access to the subsequent biography is doomed to produce a distorted picture.

It would be tempting to say that Buddha and St. Paul are not on a parity in the way the Buddha and Christ are with respect to carrying out vs. inventing the path. But it must be remembered that, simplistic textbooks and *bhakti* cult deviations aside,[28] the Buddha Gotama is not regarded as the Founder of Buddhism—only as a pathfinder in this eon. For from an emic perspective the belief is that there were previous Buddhas, and that more are to come. Since the *dhamma* is eternal, it is only from a very much more restricted time-span than is operative in early Buddhism, that Gotama is the Founder. Etically viewed against the backdrop of Hindu culture, Buddhism appears as a new religion, and yet emically the lineage claimed goes beyond recorded history. Therefore it cannot be accurately maintained that whereas Buddha invented a path, Paul was converted to an already existing one, as a basis for excluding their comparison.

In both the careers of Buddha and St. Paul after their most important religious experiences, a conviction which changes their lives is apparent in each case. Buddha claims an insight into things as they really are (*yathā bhūtaṃ*) and Paul insists that his doctrine is revealed and is no mere human invention. I do not think that religious experience *necessarily* results in a change of life. It might be impossible to tell what would have resulted if there were no religious experience, in which case one cannot attribute the change specifically to the religious experience. Also, having a religious experience might result in a confirmation of existing behavior patterns rather than a change in them, in cases where the patterns were already close to a religious ideal.

But even in the case of religious experience functioning to confirm, rather than to change, behavior patterns, having the experience matters in the person's life. It matters even if one does not know what would have happened without it, since the individual takes it as revelatory of reality itself. Sartre has said that there are no omens, or, if there are, it is we as individuals who choose what they must mean.[29] What Sartre's point reminds us is that no religious person may deny responsibility for his choosing a path on the *grounds* that the truth appeared to him in a flash. Even though Buddha and St. Paul claim that their experiences inevitably and certainly must be interpreted as they do, their holding this does not make the experience objective in the sense that a tape-recorder and television would report the event in the same way they interpret it. In contrast to mechanical reports, reports of religious experience are expressions of human experiences which matter in life.

Next I would like to discuss the relationship between rationality and following rules on the one hand, and between checking points of doctrine and 'rational faith' on the other. It is tempting to think that *saddhā* in early Buddhism must, as an *a priori* point, conform to a 'consequent to checking' pattern if it is to be 'rational', in line with the Buddhist empiricism thesis also emphasized by Jayatilleke. The conclusion would then be irresistible that, since it does not always so conform (as section I shows), it is not always 'rational'. But since rationality is not always a matter of following pre-conceived rules, as Mitchell points out, there is no need for a set of rules with which to check points of doctrine in order for *saddhā* to be rational.[30] Consequently it does not follow that those instances which do not conform to the 'consequent to checking' pattern are less than rational. A corollary of this view is that there is no primary occurrence (vs. secondary) which is taken to be the more rational type of occurrence.

Now the time is right to introduce the topic of *abhiññā* and evidence. A crucial difference between the ancient *Cārvāka* and Buddhists is expressed by Jayatilleke thus:[31]

> (285) The Materialist condemnation of the Vedic tradition, as we have shown above, was absolute. According to them the authors of the Vedas were both utterly ignorant as well as vicious; they are called 'buffoons, knaves and demons' (v. *supra*, 121) but the Buddhists held that the original seers who were the authors of the Vedas merely lacked a special insight (*abhiññā*) but did not doubt their honesty or virtue....

Here the importance of the *abhiññā* to early Buddhism is evident. Its relevance to an issue of major philosophical significance, that of the nature of religious belief, becomes clear when seen as a key concept in all those studies which favor seeing early Buddhism as a form of empiricism. According to this view the *abhiññā* supply the evidence on the basis of which points of doctrine can be confirmed. Part of the initial plausibility of this view derives from the lack of a detailed examination of *saddhā* and the consequent failure to notice that *saddhā* is not always consequent to checking. But the view of early Buddhism as grounded on evidence (provided by those who take the time and effort to master *abhiññā*) is a very important one in that it raises the question of whether religious belief can rise or fall with the evidence. Colin Lyas thinks that, as far as Christian belief is concerned, it could not, and holds his position[32]

> if true to entail certain ways of establishing beliefs are suspect when applied to the case of religious belief in God. That is why I say that as *we* use the term religion, a religious belief in God could not rise or fall with the evidence. I feel that the only way to undermine that entailment is to show that what I have said about religion is not true.

Earlier in the same symposium Norman Malcolm says that religious belief waxes and wanes, but not with the evidence. On this point he and Lyas are agreed. Could early Buddhism rightly be considered an example of a religion which *does* 'undermine that entailment' in providing an example of a religious position on which belief is regarded as appropriate only insofar as it is supported by evidence? The following examination of *abhiññā* will be helpful in answering this question.[33]

In early Buddhism the *abhiññā* are:

1. *iddhividhā* (psychokinesis)
2. *dibbasota* (clairaudience)
3. *cetopariyañāṇa* (telepathy)
4. *pubbenivāsanussatiñāṇa* (retrocognition)
5. *dibbacakkhu* (clairvoyance)
6. *āsavakkhayañāṇa* (knowledge of the destruction of defilements or *āsavas*)

Concerning these Jayatilleke says:[34]

> Of the six only three are necessary for the saving knowledge. The first is retrocognition with which he verifies the fact of pre-existence (*v. supra*, 754). The second is clairvoyance, with which he verifies the fact of karma (*v. supra*, 755). The third is the 'knowledge of the destruction of the defiling impulses' (āsavānaṃ khayañāṇa-, M.I. 348). With this he verifies the Four Noble truths (*loc. cit.*).

Hence the importance of becoming a 'three-fold knowledge' (*tisso vijjā*) adept. Not everyone who tries can attain this easily, and one passage mentions that only 60 were successful out of a group of 500.[35] As to why some monks can attain the 'three-fold knowledge' and are consequently 'freed by mind' (*cetovimutti*), while others cannot but instead are 'freed by insight (or wisdom') (*paññāvimutti*) the answer is given that this is due to a difference in their abilities (*indriyavemattataṃ*).[36] For the one freed by *paññā* Jayatilleke observes:[37]

> The doctrine of rebirth and karma and the greater part of the theory of Buddhism would have had to be accepted on faith by such a person since he did not have within him or develop the power of verifying them. This explains the conception of the saint with faith (saddhā) in the Pāli Canon....

It is still open to the advocate of 'Buddhist empiricism' to argue that *in principle,* even though not always in practice, *kamma* and *punabbhava* are verifiable.

Rather than raise conceptual and empirical difficulties at the outset about any of the *abhiññā* in particular, it is assumed for the sake of argument that these terms have some meaning in order to go on to raise the question of what verification is supposed to be here. At *Dīgha Nikāya* I.81 a passage translated by Jayatilleke runs[38]

> I was in such a place with such a personal and family name, such a status, having such and such food, such and such experiences and such a term of life. Dying there I was born in such and such a place; there too I had such a name.... Dying there I was born here.

This is compared to someone visiting various villages and recalling details of the journey. It also shows a point not emphasized by Jayatilleke, that retrocognition here concerns *one's own case* in contrast to clairvoyance which, he continues[39]

> Is directed towards gaining a knowledge of the decease and survival of beings and acquiring an understanding of karma: 'With his clear paranormal clairvoyant vision he sees beings dying and being reborn, the low and the high, the fair and the ugly, the good and the evil, each according to his karma ....'. It is also by its means that one sees contemporaneous events beyond the ken of normal vision.

It is important to notice that the quotation is not about all beings including oneself, but about *other beings.* By clairvoyance, their rebirth in accordance with a moral order concerning action (*kamma*) is supposed to be known. Keeping the underlined features in mind one turns to Jayatilleke's remark a few pages later that retrocognition 'verifies the fact of pre-existence' and clairvoyance 'verifies the fact of karma'.[40]

The inaccuracy should now be clear. The distinction is not between faculties verifying respective doctrines as Jayatilleke thinks. The texts he mentions show a distinction that goes unmentioned *viz.*, that one difference between retrocognition and clairvoyance is that the former concerns my own case and the latter that of other beings. Rebirth is thought to be seen in *both* retrocognitive and clairvoyant experience, so that 'the fact of pre-existence' is not verified exclusively by retrocognition. That *kamma* affects other beings is what is taken to distinguish clairvoyant experience here.

Concerning the last of the 'three-fold knowledge', Jayatilleke cites *Dīgha Nikāya* I. 84 where suffering, its cause, cessation and the path to its cessation (*i.e.,* the 'four noble truths') as well as the defilements, their cause, cessation, and path to their cessation (knowledge of the destruction of defilements) are known. But he links this discussion to *anumāna* which he translates 'inference' and *anvaye ñāṇaṃ* translated as 'inductive knowledge'. *Anumāna* is not just inference in general, however, although commonly translated as such, but is of the 'just as..so too...' *analogical* type. And *anvaya* (in *anvaye ñāṇaṃ*) has no specific meaning of induction, but when used with *ñāṇa* means 'logical conclusion of' according to the PTS dictionary. Jayatilleke's use of the term 'induction' is exemplified as follows:[41]

> In the Saṃyutta Nikāya are described a number of causally correlated phenomena such as that 'with the arising of birth there is the arising of decay and death, and with the cessation of birth there is the cessation of decay and death', etc. (jātisamudayā jarāmaraṇasamudayo jātinirodhā jarāmaraṇanirodho...S. II. 57). Knowing these causal correlations or sequences is called 'the knowledge of phenomena' (dhamme ñāṇam, S. II. 58). Then it is said, 'This constitutes the knowledge of phenomena; by seeing, experiencing, acquiring knowledge before long and delving into these phenomena, *he draws an inference* (nayam neti) *with regard to the past and the future* (atītānāgate, *loc., cit.*) as follows: 'All those recluses and brahmins who thoroughly understood the nature of decay and death, its cause, its cessation and the path leading to the cessation of decay and death did so in the same way as I do at present; all those recluses and

> brahmins who in the future will thoroughly understand the nature of decay and death...will do so in the same way as I do at present–*this constitutes his inductive knowledge* (idam assa anvaye ñāṇam, *loc. cit.*).

This is an argument from what is true in my own case now using certain procedures of checking to what is true irrespective of time (in past and future) for others using the same procedures. Thus, it has an analogical quality not covered just by calling it inductive.

To sum up, retrocognition is taken to reveal *kamma* (action), *phala* (consequence), *punabbhava* (rebirth) in my own case, clairvoyance to reveal *kamma, phala* and *punabbhava* in other beings' cases, and the knowledge of the destruction of *āsavas* (defilements) to reveal that what is true in my own case now is true in the past and the future for others using similar procedures. This can be said emically on the basis of textual evidence. But there is no basis for going further to say that these faculties *verify* the doctrines of rebirth and action in the strong, usual empiricist sense of 'verify' according to which falsification must be in principle possible. There is an ambiguity in the expression 'rebirth doctrine'. If taken as view in the sense of picture, in full recognition of there being no propositional sense here, then of course Buddhists have a 'doctrine'. But if taken as a theory to be defended with argument, in view of the condemnation of *diṭṭhi* as speculative view, there is no early Buddhist doctrine in that sense. It is well-known that theories of the relation between soul and body were set aside, as well as speculation on the state of the *Tathāgata*. This shows the unwillingness to become 'entangled' in a specific philosophical theory of rebirth.

What of the possibility that 'knowledge and vision' (*ñāṇa-dassana*) might play an analogous role to 'verify' in English. Consider:[42]

> It is *in the nature of things* (dhammatā) that a person in the state of (meditative) concentration knows and sees what really is. A person who knows and sees what really is, does not need to make an effort of will to feel disinterested and renounce. It is *in the*

> *nature of things* that a person who knows and sees as it really is, feels disinterested and renounces. One who has felt disinterested and has renounced does not need an effort of will to realize the knowledge and insight of emancipation (vimutti-ñāṇadassanaṃ). It is in the nature of things that one who has felt disinterested and renounced, realizes the knowledge and insight of emancipation.

Here, however, there is no mention of *kamma*, *punabbhava* or any other specific doctrine being known and seen.

There are cases where 'knowing and seeing' refers to knowledge of physical objects, as when a man cannot know and see his face in water due to the water's turbulent surface. Thus knowledge and vision is not always applied to religious concepts in the Buddhist texts. On the other hand, Jayatilleke emphasizes its religious application in saying:[43]

> Now it is said that 'the decease and survival of beings is to be verified by one's (clairvoyant) vision' (sattānaṃ cutūpapāto...cakkhunā sacchikaraṇīyo, A. II. 183). But with this clairvoyant vision one is also said to notice a correlation between the character of a person and his state of survival.

The crucial word in Pāli, *sacchikatvā* ('verified', 'seen') takes an emphatic (*yo*) form here as *sacchikaraṇīyo*. It is *prima facie* odd that this word has not been one of the Pāli terms often used in English language expositions of the Buddhist empiricism line. *Sacca* means 'true' or 'correct' (it does not distinguish between propositional/ontological), and *katvā*, 'made' or 'established'. 'True' is here not used as a property of a proposition, but as a property of utterance, congruent with the findings of Ch. 3. Since the concern of logical empiricism or positivism is with the meaning and verification of *propositions* (and often with the possibility in principle of *falsification*), the concern of early Buddhism with *sacca* cannot be the same. *Eo ipso*, *sacchikatvā* ('established') cannot refer to verification in this sort of positivist's sense.* Now it can be surmised why none in the Buddhist empiri-

*Since logical empiricism (or positivism) can take many forms, someone might argue that it may take a form which does not require the terms 'pro-

cism tradition of interpretation make much of *sacchikatvā* or its related forms: their Pāli scholarship did not let them fall into the trap of wrongly interpreting the term as relating to propositions. Perhaps they realized (as I have noted elsewhere) that there is no term for 'proposition' in early Buddhism.[44] But one must not let this crucial term pass unnoticed, and once its usage is understood, all talk of verifying propositions is ruled out.

This by itself is not, however, a sufficient argument to eliminate the Buddhist empiricism thesis, because it might be argued that even without 'the logician's notion of proposition' (which itself is not entirely free of difficulties in philosophy of logic), there may still be, and have historically been, empiricist positions. Even if reply is correct, it is of no avail against the following further considerations.

Leaving aside all claims of comparison with logical empiricism for which the notion of proposition is essential, the more restricted comparison to some form of empiricism which does not involve a notion of proposition has yet to account for the in-principle falsifiability of a 'view'. This may be seen clearly in section III when my 'parable of the *bhikkhu*' is discussed.

The following remarks are intended as a transition to section III where some further considerations against the Buddhist empiricism thesis are presented. Whether *Tathāgatas* arise or not the *dhamma* is eternal—this saying shows that the truth of a doctrinal 'view' is never regarded as contingent on man's realization: although checking is not irrelevant, it takes on a different sense from checking a proposition or hypothesis. The investigation takes the general form: P examines religion X to see if there is anything in it for him. Religious texts and believers typically make the claim that something is indeed 'in it', whether the merely curious can see it or not. This should not obscure the fact that 'religious discovery' is at least partly a matter of what the investigator is, what he 'brings with him' to the search.

If my line of thinking is correct, then it is a mistake to think that there is a body of propositions which can be rightly labeled

position' and 'falsification' such that it is compatible with early Buddhism. All I can say is that I would have to see the case made out. Doing so with reference to any historically recognizable strand of empiricism, while at the same time not distorting the religious nature of early Buddhism, is at least unlikely if not logically impossible.

'religious knowledge', in a sense even remotely analogous to scientific knowledge. Unlike 'religious knowledge', there may indeed be 'religious wisdom', but if there is, it is to be found embodied in the lives of religious people, and as with 'philosophical wisdom', cannot be defined in a set of propositions but is embodied in practices. Unlike knowledge, wisdom is thus necessarily spared the indignity of becoming a commodity.

III

In a cumulative manner this section builds upon the arguments in I concerning *saddhā* and in II concerning *abhiññā*. The crucial points established are that *saddhā* is an important element in Early Buddhist thought, and that it does not always conform to a 'consequent to checking' pattern. The interpretation of the role of *abhiññā* is pivotal for the understanding of the nature of religious belief in the Early Buddhist context. In II I have suggested that the view of *abhiññā* as epistemological basis for Early Buddhism needs to be examined, but so far have not offered arguments against this view as such. It has been argued, however, that it is textually inaccurate to say that pre-existence is verified by retrocognition. In III the view just mentioned will be examined in detail.

Elsewhere I have argued that early Buddhism is not a form of empiricism, and that consequently there is no basis for an Early Buddhist apologetic which favorably contrasts an empirical Early Buddhism with other religions such as Hinduism and Christianity.* In this section I will only briefly summarize the gist of that argument, and following on from that intend to clarify the import of my hypothetical case, the 'parable of the *bhikkhu*' (Buddhist monk). That argument is integral to sections I and II here, and in order to appreciate its full force these sections should be taken into account.

Briefly, it does not follow from the set of reasons Jayatilleke adduces, that it is a justifiable extension of the word 'empiricism' to let it include Early Buddhism. For there are both textual and philosophical considerations which Jayatilleke does not take into account in this context that militate against this extension. As for textual arguments, (1) *diṭṭhi* ('speculative views', lit. 'views') are set aside as not conducive to development on the Buddhist

*Citation provided on the following page.

path; *takka* ('argument and counter-argument') is also thought of as a hindrance to liberation. Since empiricism is a *theory* of knowledge, up for argument and counter-argument, it would not be acceptable from an *emic* ('internal') perspective as part of Early Buddhism. Is there any reason for thinking that it might be acceptable from an *etic* ('external') point of view to describe Early Buddhism as empiricism? In reply to this question some philosophical considerations need to be mentioned.

Basically, Early Buddhism cannot be empiricism in the strong sense according to which falsifiability in principle is necessary for meaning. My 'parable of the *bhikkhu*' was meant to underscore this point by illustrating how progress in understanding the nature of religious belief consists, in part, in ceasing to see it as an experimental (empirical in the strong sense) matter while seeing it as nevertheless experiential. The source of inspiration for my parable will be obvious to philosophers of religion conversant with the work of John Wisdom.* In his 'parable of the gardener' Wisdom makes much the same point in the context of Christian theism. Concerning the existence of an invisible, intangible gardener, the believer and the non-believer come to see that their disagreement is not an experimental one:[45]

> At this stage, in this context, the gardener hypothesis has ceased to be experimental, the difference between one who accepts and one who rejects it is not now a matter of the one expecting something the other does not expect.

That is, neither of the two think that their belief is a falsifiable one, for[46]

> their different words now reflect no difference as to what they have found in the garden, no difference as

*Since the publication of my parable in 'The Buddhist Empiricism Thesis' (*Religious Studies*, vol. 18, no. 2, June 1982, pp. 151-158) it has become apparent that some readers have not seen the parable as similar in form to Wisdom's 'parable of the gardener'. In acknowledging my debt to Wisdom on the point discussed above, I do not, however, wish to ascribe to any *general* theory of religious belief as 'seeing as'. A follow-up discussion may be found in the article, 'Buddhist Belief "In"', in *Religious Studies* vol. 21, pp. 381-387.

> to what they would find in the garden if they looked further and no difference about how fast unattended gardens fall into disorder.

Similarly in Buddhism, although the doctrine is a 'come and see' doctrine, it will not be falsified by the assiduous meditating monk who meditates and yet does not 'see' rebirth. If such a monk were ever dull enough to conflate meditation with a scientific hypothesis capable of falsification if false, then he will face the meditation teacher's unrelenting remonstrations to go and meditate more. At no point will the meditation teacher agree that the student has falsified the doctrine in case the student came and did not see.

From an 'external' or *etic* perspective I do not see how Buddhism can be regarded as empiricism without radically distorting the nature of religious belief. It is far from easy to give an account of the nature of religious belief, and there is no claim to do so here. But one feature of any such account must be, I would argue, a recognition of the distinction between religious belief and scientific belief. Although making this distinction is a complex task, one characteristic of distinctively religious beliefs is their unfalsifiability in principle. Of course, claims *about* religions and claims that such-and-such an event occurred are falsifiable in principle (not necessarily in practice) if false, but one needs to be careful about 'event'. 'Events' do not pertain to religious beliefs in the scientific, historical usage of that term. For example, the belief that 'Christ lived' (a distinctively religious belief) is not the same type of belief as the belief that 'Jesus lived' (a historical belief). Some people might take the latter for a religious belief, but that would be to confuse matters. Belief that Jesus the Christ rose from the dead is a religious belief which the faithful will never let counter-evidence count against. It is not falsifiable in principle, and it is just not the kind of belief that can be assigned a truth-value.

In developing a philosophical account, however incomplete, of the nature of religious belief, it is important to look at particular religions. Buddhists await the coming of Maitreya (the future Buddha) much as Christians await the Second Coming of Christ. Their hope is open-ended, and not subject to contingencies: it will be maintained come what may. When concerned with the future, religious belief often has a *prophetic,* rather than a *predictive,* quality. In order to count as 'prophetic' in this sense, such a belief does not have to be held by a prophet. The prophetic quality which future-oriented religious belief often has is distorted or overlooked if one thinks of religious belief as an experiment.

The view that ideas are *derived* from experience has nothing to do with Buddhism, for this is not a Buddhist concern. Yet this emphasis on the origin of our ideas is of crucial importance for articulating sorts of empiricism. Concept empiricism, for example, may be distinguished from empiricism *simpliciter.* Concept empiricists hold that all concepts are acquired through experience, and in this sense both Locke and Aquinas are concept empiricists. But they are not by that fact committed to the further claim that all propositions are acquired from experience, which claim Hospers uses to characterize in part empiricism as such.

Is Early Buddhism espousing a form of concept empiricism? Does it hold the view of Aquinas, say, that there is nothing in the intellect that is not first in the sense? I think not. First, there is no separation of senses and intellect in a comparable way. The Buddhist 'gateways' (*āyatana*) are six: the five sense plus the mind; the mind being considered alongside the senses rather than in contrast or opposition to them. In discussing what counts as 'everything' the *Sabbasutta* defines it as these six plus their respective objects. But nothing is said about the issue of the origin of ideas in terms of whether they derive from the senses or from reason alone. In short, I find no basis for attributing concept empiricism to Early Buddhism, anymore than empiricism as such.

The next chapter raises another key issue for the interpretation of mind in Early Buddhism: how is *amata* ('the deathless') to be understood without the supposition of a permanent, unchanging mental substratum?

NOTES

[1]On the last mentioned distinction see K. N. Jayatilleke, *Early Buddhist Theory of Knowledge* (London: Allen & Unwin, 1963), p. 393.

[2]I.B. Horner (trans.), *The Middle Length Sayings* (London: Luzac and Co. for the Pāli Text Society, 1967) vol. III, p. 85.

[3]Horner, *op. cit.*, MLS vol. II, p. 365.

[4]*Saṃyutta Nikāya* II, XII, 23, 9, '*yathābhūtaññāṇadassananassa*'.

[5]*Gradual Sayings* III, 7, 65.

[6]F.L. Woodward (trans.), *Kindred Sayings* (*Saṃyutta Nikāya*) (London: Pāli Text Society, 1979), p. 180.

[7]Rhys Davids and Stede, *op. cit.*, p. 675.

[8]*Majjhima Nikāya* (MN) I, 509); *Middle Length Sayings* (*MLS*) II, 189. The translation here in *MLS* has 'faith'.

[9]*Cf. MN* III, 23 (*MLS* III, 73); *MN* III, 21 (*MLS* III, 71).

[10]*MN* I, 444: '*pema*' as 'regard or affection'. *MN* III, 6 (*MLS* III, 56).

[11]*MN* I, 463 (*MLS* II, 135).

[12]*MN* I, 465 (*MLS* II, 138).

[13]*MN* II, 185. 'Faith is the seed (*bīja*)', *Kindred Sayings* I, 217.

[14]*Vide MN* I, 67 for *saddhā* in Buddha and *dhamma* only, *MN* I, 57 for *saddhā* in *dhamma* by itself, and *MN* I, 479 for *saddhā* in the *Tathāgata*.

[15]*MN* I, 479 (*MLS* II, 154).

[16]Jayatilleke, *ibid.*, p. 373.

[17]Jayatilleke, *ibid.*, p. 389.

[18]Stewart R. Sutherland, 'St. Paul's Damascus Experience' in *Sophia* (Australia, 1975), p. 15.

[19]*Ibid.*, p. 13.

[20]*Ibid.*, p. 13.

[21]*Ibid.*, p. 15.

[22]Jayatilleke, *op. cit.*, p. 324; *Dīgha Nikāya* I, pp. 212-213.

[23]*Udāna*, p. 1.

[24]Basil Mitchell, *The Justification of Religious Belief* (London: Macmillan, 1973), p. 91. He then goes on to argue that rational choice is still possible here, for there is no need to think that reasoning is necessarily in accordance with rules which vary from one system to another.

[25]David J. Kalupahana, *Buddhist Philosophy* (Honolulu: University of Hawaii Press, 1976), p. 7. Kalupahana's way of understanding the distinctiveness of the Buddhist view of *āsavas* is helpful.

[26]E. J. Thomas, *A History of Buddhism* (London: Routledge & Kegan Paul, 1971 edition), p. 13.

[27]Sutherland, *op. cit.*, p. 15.

[28]*Vide* B.M. Barua, 'Faith in Buddhism' in Bimala C. Law, *Buddhistic Studies* (Calcutta: Thacker, 1931). He observes that the commentator Buddhaghosa defines faith in such a way as to being it close to the Hindu concept of *bhakti* (p. 332).

[29]Jean-Paul Sartre: 'No general ethics can show you what is to be done; there are no omens in the world. The Catholics will reply, "But there are." Granted—but, in any case, I myself choose the meaning they have'. Cited in E. Sprague and P. Taylor (eds.), *Knowledge and Value* (New York: Harcourt, 1967), pp. 612-613.

[30]Mitchell, *ibid.*

[31]Jayatilleke, *ibid.*, p. 188.

[32]S. C. Brown (ed.), *Reason and Religion* (Cornell University Press, 1977), p. 178.

[33]Jayatilleke, *op. cit.*, p. 438 presents a roughly similar schema.

[34]*Ibid.*, p. 466.

[35]*Ibid.*, p. 467.

[36]*Ibid.*

[37]*Ibid.*

[38]*Ibid.*, p. 440. Incorrectly cited as D I 82 by Jayatilleke, this passage is translated with minor variations in F. Max Müller, *Dialogues of the Buddha* vol. II (London: Pāli Text Society, 1977), Sacred Books of the Buddhists Series, p. 90.

[39]*Ibid.*, p. 441.

[40]*Ibid.*, p. 466.

[41]*Ibid.*, pp. 442-443.

[42]*Ibid.*, pp. 420-421.

[43]*Ibid.*, p. 460.

[44]A discussion of this point occurs in my article 'Early Buddhist Four Fold Logic' in *Journal of Indian Philosophy* (10) 1982, p. 327.

[45]"Gods", first published in *Proceedings of the Aristotelian Society* (London, 1944-1945). Reprinted in *Logic and Language*, I. ed. Antony Flew (Oxford: Basil Blackwell, and New York: Mott Ltd., 1951); in John Wisdom, *Philosophy and Psychoanalysis* (Oxford: Basil Blackwell, and New York: Mott Ltd., 1953), pp. 154-155; and in Jonn Hick, ed., *Classical and Contemporary Readings in the Philosophy of Religion* (Englewood Cliffs, N.J.: Prentice-Hall, Inc., 2nd ed., 1970).

[46]*Ibid.*

CHAPTER 6

THE DEATHLESS (*AMATA*)

The problem of the reidentification of the person across lives discussed in Ch. 4 cannot be solved by appeal to the Buddhist empiricism thesis, as Ch. 5 shows. But in rejecting this thesis it is not being claimed that *parinibbāna* is a 'transcendent state'. How, then, does one interpret 'the deathless' (*amata*) in early Buddhism? This is the problem to be solved in the present chapter.

Some writers on Early Buddhist 'immortality' see it as easily assimilable to a religion they admire, such as Hinduism or Christianity. For example, Radhagovinda Basak writes:[1]

> It is, indeed, very interesting to find in the Buddhist canons this *nirvāṇa* described as a-kata (akṛta, the uncreated) and amata (amṛta, the immortal), *i.e.* it is neither created, nor does it ever die. Hence, it may be presumed that it is a *siddhavastu*, eternally existing thing, and it may be equated with the Brahmanic idea of Brahman.

Whether the 'eternally existing thing' is thought of in Hindu or in Christian terms, there is no such thing in Buddhism. This much can be seen already, in the light of Ch. 4, but it is the contention of the present chapter that *amata* nevertheless has a clear Buddhist meaning. To explain what meaning 'the deathless' has in Early Buddhism which is different from the notion of something which never dies (N.B. Basak's way of construing 'eternal'), it is necessary initially to look at the texts. In doing so the conventional distinction between *nibbāna* and *parinibbāna* is used here, and is defended against a recent attack by Peter Masefield. The argument developed here on a textual basis is that *amata* means 'immortal' in the sense of 'eternal life' and not in the sense of 'endless life', as these senses of 'immortality' are distinguished in some contemporary philosophy of religion. It is also demonstrated how misinterpretations of *amata* as 'endless life persist down to the present day in writers like Kalansuriya.

Although elucidating the Early Buddhist position may make it easier to accept, the concern is not with acceptance but with understanding, as pointed out in the Introduction. And in making comparisons between what the texts say and what philosophy of religion works say, the comparisons are not regarded as valuable somehow in their own right, nor as causal influence accounts, not as concealed apologetics to make Buddhism seem respectable (for the view taken is that it *is* respectable), but only for the sake of understanding. If it turns out that there is some clarity in the Buddhist vision (along with some difficulties), this should not be surprising, nor taken as evidence of apologetic intent. Hence, if the philosophy of religion can on some points aid understanding without doing violence to the texts, the absence of exact Pāli equivalents to its distinctions (say, between 'endless' and 'eternal' life as two kinds of 'immorality') will be excusable as a matter of course.

With this methodological reminder concluded, consider some uses of '*amata*' in the *Nikāya* literature. The *PTS dictionary* characterizes *amata* as 'the drink of the gods, ambrosia, water of immortality', and in painstaking manner details its usages. What follows is not meant as an exhaustive summary, but is sufficiently developed for present purposes.

'*Amata*' is used as a synonym for '*nibbāna*', and as shorthand for 'the destruction of passion, hatred, and confusion' (*rāga*, *dosa*, and *moha*). There are expressions like knocking at the 'door of the deathless' (*dvārāmata*), and knowing the causal relation is sometimes said to be a prerequisite of knocking at that door. The deathless is sometimes characterized as the purification of *citta* free of grasping, and sometimes it is said that 'purposive thoughts' (*saṅkappa-vitakka*, AN IV 385) are merged in the deathless. Some thoughts are said to be particularly beneficial for attaining the deathless. Also found are expressions like 'plunging into the deathless', and 'the deathless way to peace', and the 'drum of deathlessness'. '*Amata*' is called 'an element', 'security', a 'quarter' (although this last is metaphorical, not spatial), and the Buddha is styled 'giver of the deathless', and 'teaching the deathless path'. Buddhists take the deathless as goal or consummation, and it must be 'seen for oneself'.

'*Amata*' as end or goal may be a synonym for '*nibbāna*', but in some places like the following it is an attribute of *nibbāna*:[2]

> Yathā asaṅkhataṃ tathā vitthāretabbaṃ tatruddānam asaṅkhatam antam anāsavam saccañca pāram nipuṇaṃ sududdasaṃ ajajjarantaṃ dhuvam apalokitaṃ anidassanaṃ nippapañca santaṃ amataṃ paṇītañca sivañca khemaṃ taṇhakkhayo acchariyañca abbhutam anītikam anitīkadhammaṃ nibbānam etaṃ sugatena desitaṃ.

K.N. Upadhyaya translates this passage as:[3]

> This is the Nibbāna, the uncompounded, *the ultimate*, free from defilements, *the truth, the further shore, the subtle,* very difficult to see, the unfading, *the stable*, the undecaying, the ineffable, the undifferentiated, *the peaceful,* the deathless, *the excellent, the good, the security,* destruction of craving, *the wonderful, the marvellous,* free from ill, the state free from ill, the harmless, the passionless, *the purity,* the release, the non-attachment, *the island, the cave, the protection, the refuge* and *the goal* which the well-accomplished One has taught.

To begin our discussion it is important to distinguish between *nibbāna* in one's lifetime from *nibbāna* at death in the case where one will not return (*i.e.*, *parinibbāna*). The objective is to explain what meaning the deathless has which is different from that of something that never dies, and this turns on the understanding of *parinibbāna*. Kalansuriya sets out 'two views of *nibbāna*' and argues for Jayatilleke's notion of *nibbāna* (perhaps also *parinibbāna*, although this is unclear), as against Kalupahana's view of *parinibbāna* as extinction.[4] In so doing he seems to think that throwing doubt on the latter's Buddhist empiricism view lends support to his own view. While not agreeing to the Buddhist empiricism thesis, I hope to show that Kalupahana is more nearly correct on the question of extinction, and why, strictly speaking, neither the transcendental state view nor the extinction view is in keeping with Buddhism.

Nowhere in the literature of the *Nikāyas* does the Buddha assert any view about the afterlife of the *Tathāgata*. In the discussion of the four-fold logic it was shown in Ch. 2 that the Early

Buddhist view is to set aside from consideration, but without denying, the four recognized possibilities concerning the *Tathāgata*. Simply put, there is a refusal to philosophize about the matter, for philosophy is seen as just another source of attachment.

Kalansuriya calls attention to a *Saṃyutta Nikāya* passage which is as important as it is occasionally misleading—one sometimes referred to as 'Yamaka's *diṭṭhi*'. It reminds one that, rightly stated, the early Buddhist view is not precisely that the *Tathāgata* is extinct after death, but that the five aggregates are *dukkha* and are all destroyed on the *Tathāgata*'s death. Yamaka, under questioning by Buddha, changes his tune from the former to the latter characterization. In the English paraphrase there is a problem with 'extinct', since *nibbāna* is sometimes rendered as 'extinction' where *parinibbāna* is meant, and of course the Buddhists are perfectly willing to say that a *Tathāgata* may be in *parinibbāna*. But in the sense in which one commonly uses 'extinction' to mark the going out of existence, the Buddhists do not *say* that the *Tathāgata* is extinct. Hence, if one emphasizes the importance of Yamaka's *diṭṭhi* and ignore others like the *Sabbasutta,* it may seem as if the door to the deathless swings open to a 'transcendental state' of existence.

In commenting on Yamaka's *diṭṭhi* Kalansuriya takes it that the Buddha *denies* the conclusion that 'once the external object (the external person) ceases to exist, ontologically, nothing exists', and at the end of the day the way to see Buddha's denial that he is an annihilationist is to see him as an eternalist, only not an Upaniṣadic eternalist. An examination of the following citations bears this out:[5]

> To put it yet more explicitly, the dissolution of the aggregation is but the non-existence of the object or person or whatever is referred to. Characteristically, this is the knowledge which comes by way of sense-experience (sense-perception). Once the external object (the external person) ceases to exist, ontologically, nothing exists. It is this conclusion that the Buddha denies, according to the Nikāya literature, when he was charged with being an annihilationist with reference to the summum bonum—nibbāna, of his teaching. The Buddha claims that

> he lays down simply a doctrine about anguish and the stopping of anguish and not the cutting off, the destruction and the disappearance of the existent entity. Therefore, we conclude that Kalupahana's reading of the meanings of advanced Western thought into the Dhamma of Buddhism is uncalled for. It is worth being clear about this since it will clarify the logical status of the notion of nibbāna in the Dhamma....
>
> From a rejection of metaphysics (that is, the eternalistic metaphysics of the Upaniṣadic seers) on the one hand, and from a rejection on the other hand of materialistic empiricism, it does not follow necessarily that all metaphysical views are rejected. A metaphysical theory about nibbāna very different from that of the Upaniṣadic ātman is not necessarily foreign to the central notions of the Dhamma.

Here 'denies', 'external person', and 'not necessarily foreign' require scrutiny. Kalansuriya thinks the Buddha (or the Buddhist position) *denies* the statement: 'once the external object (the external person) ceases to exist, ontologically, nothing exists.' There are a number of considerations here. The text does not depict Buddha as denying this in explaining Yamaka's *diṭṭhi*. Perhaps Kalansuriya takes it that annihilationism (*ucchedavāda*) is correctly described in the statement above, and that Buddha is depicted as denying it. He does not mention the *Sabbasutta*, however, and can hardly be unaware that Kalupahana lays a great deal of emphasis on it.[6] There, a statement like that which Kalansuriya takes an annihilationism is *asserted* (leaving aside the odd usage of 'external'). If Kalansuriya is to make a case for his view, he would have to supply an interpretation of the *Sabbasutta* or somehow argue that it is less important than Kalupahana thinks. But as he has done neither of these things, one cannot feel any the wiser by being confronted with a different text, that on Yamaka's *diṭṭhi*, thereby diverting attention from the *Sabbasutta* while not explaining the discrepancy between his statement of what the Buddha denies and what the *Sabbasutta* actually asserts.

On my reading of Early Buddhism one has to interpret *uccheda-*

vāda very differently from Kalansuriya. Interpreted as the view of *Cārvāka* that there is no rebirth, that at death one is completely destroyed ('the cutting off of an existent entity' is the phrase), the Buddha's insistence that he only illuminates suffering and the way to the eradication of suffering makes a good deal of sense. It is then really a middle path in the sense of an alternative between Hindu eternalism of the Upaniṣads and the materialism of *Cārvāka*. On the view I suggest, there is no difficulty reconciling the *Sabbasutta* with Yamaka's *diṭṭhi*, such as Kalansuriya would encounter if he confronted it. Since annihilationism is, *pace* Kalansuriya, not the statement he presents but that there is no rebirth or transmigration of any sort, the Buddha's unwillingness to accept it and concern to clarify what he *does* say—I preach *dukkha* and its cessation—does not in any way conflict with the *Sabbasutta* passage.

I have already given reasons for opposing the Buddhist empiricism thesis. Thus I am in agreement with Kalansuriya's conclusion, on this particular point, although not with his argument for his conclusion. For as that argument misinterprets *ucchedavāda* and slurs the logical independence of the Buddhist empiricism thesis and the *parinibbāna* as extinction thesis, it is unacceptable as an argument, however much one may agree with its conclusion. If my arguments are correct, then the former thesis is unacceptable, while the latter (on *parinibbāna*) is acceptable in a qualified manner as an implication of the Early Buddhist doctrine, but not as a paraphrase of what is explicitly said in Pāli. That is, there is no place in the *Nikāya* literature where the Buddha is depicted as saying 'parinibbāna is extinction'. On the other hand, he says that rebirth depends on conditions and that when the conditions are not there no rebirth occurs; that it would be absolute, complete folly to assert the continuance of any mind-related element under such circumstances. That *parinibbāna* is extinction is an etic interpretation, not an emic view of Early Buddhism *per se*.

II

Part of the argument of the preceding section turns on the distinction between *nibbāna* and *parinibbāna*, and it is the defense of this distinction from a recent attack that is now undertaken.

Peter Masefield argues that while there is some textual evidence for the above-mentioned distinction, the distinction cannot be maintained. He writes:[7]

> Had the expression parinibbāna and its related terms been found only in such contexts one might have been justified in assuming that parinibbāna was always and only to be attained at death. Other passages, however, suggest that one already parinibbuto (9) could continue to live and remain active in the world; it is said, for instance, in the Udumbarika-Sīhanāda Sutta that the Lord, himself parinibbuta teaches Dhamma for the sake of (the attainment of) pariniābbna (10), which must surely imply that at the time he was neither dead nor dying. Similarly several passages elsewhere, dealing with those either attaining parinibbāna or already parinibbuta, give no reason for us to suppose that the individuals in question are either dying or already dead (11).

And he supports this with notes:[8]

> 9. Past participle of parinibbayati and thus 'who has attained nibbāna'.
> 10. Parinibbuto so Bhagavā parinibbānāya dhammaṃ deseti—D iii 55.
> 11. See *e.g.* S iv 204; Sn 514 etc.

The choice of topic here is an ingenious one, for if it could be shown that there is no distinction operative here, then an important contribution to Buddhist scholarship would be made. Nevertheless the argument is unsound, for the following reasons.

First, nothing at (10) guarantees the implication 'that at the time he was neither dead nor dying'. For (10), which may be translated as 'Completely enlightened the Blessed One teaches doctrine for enlightenment' does not mean in context that Buddha is somehow alive and teaching. It means that the doctrine is taught in the Buddha's life. One can mean this and say that he *teaches* the way by example, just as one can say that Thomas More teaches the importance of conscience even if one has no thoughts of heaven and of More's continued existence. Since the Pāli does not guarantee Masefield's implication, then one need not agree that there is 'no reason for us to suppose that the individuals in question are either dying or already dead.' On my reading, the present tense of *deseti* is being used in a way which does not imply that Buddha is alive.

There may be other passages which Masefield is thinking of (see 11, '*etc.*'), but the ones supplied at 11 are no more compelling than *D* iii. 55. *S* iv. 204 runs thus:

> Yatha cetā nirujjhanti maggañca khayagāminam
> Vedanānam khayā bhikkhu
> nicchāto parinibbuto ti.

This has been translated as:[9]

> They cease, and what the way to feelings' end.
> That brother who hath ended them, therefore
> No longer hungereth. He is set free.

The context is that one who has eliminated pleasant, painful, and neutral feelings (*vedanā*) is *parinibbuto*. 'Set free' should not be taken as free in a relative sense (from something), where what is set free can go on existing. For Buddhist *parinibbāna* is not freedom from this or that particular condition, but 'freedom' in an extended sense—freedom from *all* conditions. And talk of one who has eliminated pleasant, painful, *and neutral* feelings is not evidence that such a one is alive.

The other passage adduced as evidence, *Sutta Nipāta* 514, goes as follows:

> Pajjena katena attanā
> parinibbānagato vitiṇṇakaṅkho,
> vibhavañ ca bhavañ ca vippahāya,
> vusitavā khīṇapunabbhavo,—sa "bhikkhu".

Lanman's translation reads:[10]

> The 'Almsman true' is he
> who treads his chosen path

> up to Nirvana, quit
> of doubts, not troubling if
> life closes or runs on,
> —the man who greatly lived
> and now hath slain rebirth.

Here the fact that rebirth is ended shows that *parinibbāna* in the usual sense as death of an Arahant is meant. There is no implication that he is actually 'in' *parinibbāna* while alive, but rather (as the translation shows), he has gone 'up to' this limit and has no concern for his own continuance.

It is not necessary to trace the other arguments Masefield gives concerning Buddhaghosa, the commentator, since I am just interested in safeguarding the *nibbāna/parinibbāna* distinction in Early Buddhism. This defense does not, however, involve the claim that '*parinibbāna*' is only used as 'death of an Arahant'. As Gombrich observes:[11]

> In Pāli literature *parinibbāna* is sometimes as synonym of *nibbāna* (technically called *sa-upādi-sesa*); but modern Sinhalese usage, to which I have conformed, confines it to the death of an *arhat* (technically *an-upādi-sesa*).

Agreeing here with Gombrich I think that even if Masefield's arguments were successful, that would not show that *in the sense in which parinibbāna means death of an arahat* 'the attainment of parinibbāna need not always entail the death of the individual concerned'. And to say:[12]

> Now, that one could attain parinibbāna and yet continue to live suggests that the distinction between the state attained by an enlightened person during his lifetime and the state attained by such an individual at his death cannot be maintained, or at least when this distinction is expressed in terms of nibbāna and parinibbāna.

is to vitiate the point by the last mentioned qualification ('or...'). For it may be admitted that sometimes '*parinibbāna*' is used synonymously with '*nibbāna*' so that the distinction is not between *nibbāna and parinibbāna simpliciter,* but between *nibbāna*- and one sense of *parinibbāna* (to which it is contrasted as 'death of an Arahat'). That is all that needs to be maintained. From the statement that one could attain *parinibbāna*$_1$ and live, it does not follow that there is no distinction to be maintained between *nibbāna* and *parinibbāna*$_2$ (where P_2 = 'death after the last lifespan of an Arahant').[13]

Given that there is a use of *parinibbāna* according to which it is applied to a living being, it does not follow that it is not used in a different way in contrast to *nibbāna*. Masefield argues that the distinction 'cannot be maintained'. In fact, the *nibbāna/parinibbāna* distinction *is* maintained, not only in contemporary Sri Lankan usage (as Gombrich observes), but in the *Nikāyas* themselves. The underlying assumption of Masefield's view on the matter seems to be that if one can show any instances counter to the general employment of '*parinibbāna*' in opposition to '*nibbāna*', such that it is sometimes used synonymously with *nibbāna*, then there is no distinction between the two. This is to treat the labyrinth of language as if it had to conform to the logician's 'real definition'. Quite independently of particular textual data, this is a specious argument, for from the fact that a word, N, is sometimes used synonymously with P_1, it does not follow that there is no usage where N is contrasted with the other word in a different sense, P_2.

A good example to support my point concerns the use of the word *diṭṭhi*. It is sometimes used just to mean 'view', even a correct view, and often to mean 'speculative view' in opposition to the *dhamma* which is according to 'right view' (*sammā-diṭṭhi*). But from the fact that it is sometimes used in contexts where the view referred to is a 'right view', it does not follow that there is no opposition between *diṭṭhi* and *dhamma* in the way in which these terms are often opposed.

III

Using the distinction between *nibbāna* and *parinibbāna* defended in II, what does *amata* mean as applied to *nibbāna*? In the following important passage the meaning of 'the deathless' is explained so that it is clear that 'endless life' is not meant:[14]

> Savatthi was the occasion...
> Then a certain monk...said this to the Exalted One:
> '"The restraint of lust, the restraint of hatred, the restraint of illusion,'' lord, is the saying. Pray, lord, what does this restraint imply?' 'It implies, monk, the realm of Nibbāna. By it is meant the destruction of the āsavas.'
> At these words that monk said to the Exalted One: "The deathless! The deathless" lord, is the saying. Pray, lord, what is the deathless, and what the way to the deathless?'
> "That which is the destruction of lust, the destruction of hatred, the destruction of illusion, monk, that is called "the deathless". This same Ariyan eightfold way is the way to the deathless; to wit, right view...and the rest...right concentration.

Here 'the deathless' is simply the destruction of what defiles: passion, hatred, and confusion (*rāga*, *dosa*, *moha*). This applies to *nibbāna*, and now I would like to take up the question, what is meant by *amata* in case *parinibbāna* is alluded to by this term?

In answering this question it is necessary to articulate an important conclusion, arguments for which have been provided in Ch. 4. I conclude that those who think that Early Buddhism holds a belief in an immortal (in the sense of 'endless') psychic something, *which exists in a transcendental state after* $parinibbāna_2$ *is reached*, are mistaken.

Following on from this my task now becomes one of giving some answer to the question just posed which is consistent with the texts and also makes sense philosophically. A word about 'consistent with the texts': I do not mean that the texts set forth in unambiguous terms the particular interpretation which is to be given here, but that this interpretation which follows is nowhere contradicted by the texts and that textual evidence such as the above rules out alternative readings, such as *ātmavāda*. As for 'makes sense philosophically', there, too, certain things are ruled out. For the identity and conceivability problems of the view of immortality as 'endless life' are insurmountable,[15] so that this would not be a live option to consider even if, counterfactually, the Early Buddhist position embraced a view of 'endless life'.

These problems are real ones for the Early Buddhist 'rebirth link' view (as mentioned in Ch. 5), but they do not apply to *parinibbāna* as understood below.

Armed with these provisos I want to consider a remark from James Van Evra's article, 'On Death as a Limit':[16]

> Pressing the analogy then: if my life has no end in *just the way* that my visual field has no limit, then it must be in the sense that I can have no experience of death, conceived as the complete cessation of experience and thought. That is, if life is considered to be a series of experiences and thoughts, then it is impossible for me to experience death, for to experience something is to be alive, and hence to be inside the bound formed by death.

Parinibbāna functions as a limit in an analogous way, I submit, only here it is the death of an *arahat*—not just any death—that counts as the *limit* of life, for life in early Buddhism is thought to continue often from death to rebirth. The distinction between the process of dying and death as a limit parallels that between *nibbāna* and *parinibbāna*, with the differences that *nibbāna* is 'dying to the world' rather than dying *simpliciter*, and *parinibbāna* is the limit of a 'person's' experience when conceived in the Early Buddhist way. Dying is, but death is not, a process which can be experienced. And the depiction of *parinibbāna par excellence,* that of the Buddha, shows him lying prone in death, rather than dying convoluted with involuntary stomach pains due to Cunda the blacksmith's food offering. *Parinibbāna*, in the sense in which the term is contrasted with *nibbāna*, is the *limit* of a Buddhist stream of life, not an experience in that stream.

When '*amata*' is predicated of *nibbāna* (as in the salient text in Section I), this is not tantamount to asserting the utterance 'the Tathāgata exists after death', but instead is to deny that the word '*mata*' ('dead', opposite of '*amata*') applies to the *Tathāgata*. The *Tathāgata* leaves no tracks, is traceless, but not because he has invisible feet. Rather, ended is *saṃsāra* for the former person (collection of five *khandha*), where *saṃsāra* has attributes which do not apply to *nibbāna*. How precisely can immortality in Early Buddhism be understood?

Light from contemporary philosophy of religion along with sensitive textual analysis can together, I think, make very plain the sense in which immortality applies in Early Buddhism. The sense in which 'the deathless' applies in Early Buddhism may be elucidated by extrapolating from Sutherland's treatment of immortality in the Christian tradition.[17] Opting for neither of the two traditional views of immortality as disembodied consciousness or as resurrection of the body, he develops an alternative one. Sutherland claims that the belief in immortality is indeed a Christian belief, thus separating himself from those (like John Hick) who take the resurrection of the body view as primary and the immortality of the soul as a Greek accretion. Yet he reinterprets what this 'immortality' means so as to rule out of consideration the disembodied consciousness view.

With a respectful nod in the direction of Kierkegaard ('only in the ethical is there immortality in eternal life'), Sutherland goes on to develop the idea that 'immortality', taken in the sense of 'eternal life' rather than 'endless life', means not mortal, not limited by death. A belief in eternal life is, then, a belief that it is possible to live in such a way that one is not limited by, but is independent of, death. What kind of independence Kierkegaard is claiming obtains here? Sutherland suggests: one can make one's life have an *in itself* ethical dimension. One is not vulnerable to chance or change in living in this way.

There will doubtless be those who are unconvinced and who wish to interpret not just *nibbāna* in this life but *parinibbāna* also as some sort of 'transcendental state'. It is not clear whether Kalansuriya wants to go this far or just to interpret *nibbāna* in this life as transcendental. He sets out 'two views of *nibbāna*' and argues for Jayatilleke's interpretation of *nibbāna* as extinction. In this kind of talk it is sometimes not clear whether the *nibbāna* of a living adept is called 'transcendent' or that of the *Arahat*. In the former case it illuminates nothing whatsoever to use this word, and in the latter case it smacks, perversely, of the eternalism set aside by the Buddha. In what follows I argue that neither of the 'two views of *nibbāna*' is acceptable, and that Kalupahana's view is the more nearly correct one on this point.

Nowhere in the Early Buddhist literature does the Buddha assert any thesis about the afterlife of the *Tathāgata*. As previously discussed, he is shown as setting aside from consideration, without denying, the four possibilities *viz.*, that the *Tathāgata* exists after death, does not, both exists in part and does not in respect to another part, and neither exists nor does not exist (as 'exists' does not apply). Simply, on the Early Buddhist position one does not philosophize about matter, because philosophizing is just another source of attachment. It is worth noticing that the fourth alternative, set aside by the Buddha, is compatible with the 'transcendental state' view of *nibbāna.* This fact should make one cautious of accepting that view, but is not by itself reason enough for rejecting it.

Although the early texts do not assert a philosophical view of the afterlife of a *Tathāgata*, there are textual considerations which point to the conclusion that, if one is to state from an etic viewpoint what the Early Buddhist position on $parinibbāna_2$* *suggests* (but does not explicitly state), then one should say that it suggests the *Tathāgata*'s extinction rather than his continued existence. For first, the Early Buddhist view takes it that the person is a composite of five aggregates (*khandhas*), while taking *nibbāna* as not a composite of any kind (*asaṅkhata*). And consciousness (*viññāṇa*) depends on conditions, in such a way that when the conditions are absent there is no consciousness.[18] This passage, by the way, is one which Kalansuriya ignores in the article cited, and is one which gives Kalupahana's view much of its plausibility.

Secondly, it is clear that nothing could 'survive in' $parinibbāna_2$, since anything which exists is compounded, conditioned, and part of the saṁsāric wheel of becoming, and hence plagued with *dukkha*, none of which could be true of the *Tathāgata* after death. Thus, the Early Buddhist position is to be precisely stated from an emic perspective as there is *dukkha* and its cessation (more fully in terms of the four noble truths, the last of which dovetails into the eightfold noble path), rather than in terms of any thesis about the afterlife of a *Tathāgata.* Yet from an etic perspective the Early Buddhist position does *suggest* that there is no question of anything surviving in *parinibbāna* once the conditions for rebirth are gone. Consequently, if anyone wants to know (as Yamaka did) what the early position on the *Tathāgata's* continued existence after death is, the correct answer is that from an emic perspective there is none, since the question is not addressed pro or contra, but instead in keeping with the middle

*See pp. 111-112.

path (in one sense of that ideal), the emphasis is on *dukkha* and ending it. And if anyone wants to know what the early position suggests about the possibility of an immortal life in the sense of 'endless life' for the *Tathāgata*, one may point out from an etic perspective that there is no question of anything existing as nothing remains.

Why, then, does one *not* find the early texts explicitly saying that *parinibbāna*$_2$ is extinction? First, I think that the answer to this lies in the persistent, religiously-oriented intention to avoid putting forth philosophical views up for argument and counter-argument, repeatedly expressed in Early Buddhism. Secondly, since *Cārvāka* believes that extinction occurs, and since Early Buddhism (by contrast with *Cārvāka*) *suggests* that extinction must be earned by adherence to a religious path, it may have been thought important not to state the latter point explicitly in order to avoid any possibility of a wrong-headed confusion of Early Buddhism with *Cārvāka*. Thirdly, it is a conceptual, philosophical point (not an empirical one about unverifiability) that if *parinibbāna*$_2$ is extinction, then one cannot (logically) experience both sides of this limit. Thus in one's own case there is no question of being able to 'experience extinction' (as opposed to becoming extinct), and knowledge of the end of rebirth in the case of *other* beings would have to be distinguished from the sort of knowledge involved in one's own case.

In conclusion, 'the deathless' (*amata*) when applied to *nibbāna* is just the destruction of passion, hatred, and confusion (*rāga*, *dosa*, and *moha*) in the life of the living Buddhist adept. If it is thought of as applied to *parinibbāna*, as Basak implies in the quotation with which section I here began, nothing in the texts justifies thinking of it as an everlasting thing or transcendental state. As for *parinibbāna*$_2$, it could be *amata* only in the sense of being a *limit* of the flux of rebirth, as the death—not the process of dying—of an *Arahat*. The deathless does not in either case involve belief in immortality as 'endless life', but only as 'eternal life', in Sutherland's sense.

Concluding Remark

The conclusion in outline is that although internal (emic) and external (etic) understanding are not mutually exclusive (Ch. 1), and Early Buddhism is neither logically (Ch. 2) nor emotively flawed fundamentally (Ch. 3), there is a problem with the reidentification of the person on its view of rebirth (Ch. 4). This problem cannot be dispelled by appeal to the Buddhist empiricism thesis, according to which one properly trained can 'see' rebirth (Ch. 5). But in rejecting the Buddhist empiricism thesis it is not being suggested that *parinibbāna* is a 'transcendent state', for it may be understood as 'eternal life', rather than as 'endless life', in a way which does not conflict with the *anattā* doctrine (Ch. 6).

NOTES

[1]Radhagovinda Basak, *Lectures on Buddha and Buddhism* (Calcutta, Sambodhi Publications, 1961), p. 110.

[2]*Saṃyutta Nikāya* IV, p. 373.

[3]K. N. Upadhyaya, *Early Buddhism and the Bhagavad Gītā* (Delhi, Motilal Banarsidas, 1971), p. 341.

[4]A. D. P. Kalansuriya, 'Two Modern Sinhalese Views of Nibbāna' in *Religion* (London: Routledge and Kegan Paul), vol. 9, Spring 1979, pp. 1-11.

[5]*Ibid.*, pp. 3 and 5.

[6]D. J. Kalupahana, 'A Buddhist Tract on Empiricism' in *Philosophy East & West* 19 (1969), pp. 65-67. Also mentioned repeatedly in his *Buddhist Philosophy*, pp. 23 and 158.

[7]Peter Masefield, 'The Nibbana-Parinibbana Controversy' in *Religion* vol. 9, Autumn 1979, p. 216.

[8]*Ibid.*

[9]F. L. Woodward (trans.), *Kindred Sayings* (London: Pāli Text Society, 1980), vol. IV, p. 136.

[10]Lanman (trans.), *Sutta Nipāta* (Discourse Collection), *Harvard Oriental Series* vol. 37, p. 123.

[11]Richard Gombrich, *Precept and Practice* (Oxford: Clarendon Press, 1971), p. 70, fn. 14.

[12]Masefield, *ibid.*, p. 217.

[13]A. P. Buddhadatta (Maha Thera), *Concise Pāli-English Dictionary* (Colombo: The Colombo Apothecaries' Co., Ltd., 1968), p. 172.

[14]*Saṃyutta Nikāya* V, 8; of. Woodward's translation V, 7.

[15]*Vide* Stewart R. Sutherland, 'Immortality and Resurrection' in John Donnelly (ed.), *Language, Metaphysics, and Death* (New York: Fordham University Press, 1978), pp. 196-207, reprinted from *Religious Studies* 3, 1967-68, pp. 377-389.

[16]James Van Evra, 'On Death as a Limit' in John Donnelly, *op. cit.*, p. 26.

[17]Stewart R. Sutherland, 'What Happens After Death?' in *Scottish Journal of Theology* 22 (1969).

[18]*Majjhima Nikāya* I, pp. 256-257.

SELECTED BIBLIOGRAPHY

I. *Books*

Ayer, A.J., *The Concept of a Person*, London, MacMillan, 1968.

Bapat, P.V., *Vimuttimagga and Visuddhimagga*, Poona, 1937.

Barua, B. M., 'Faith in Buddhism' in Bimal C.L aw, *Buddhistic Studies*, Calcutta, Thacker, 1931.

Basak, Radhagovinda, *Lectures on Buddha and Buddhism*, Calcutta, Sambodhi Publications, 1961.

Bharati, Agehananda, *The Tantric Tradition*, London, Rider & Co., 1965.

Bleeker, C. J. and Widengren, G. (eds.), *Historia Religionum*, Leiden, E. J. Brill, 1969.

Borger, R. and Cioffi, F., *Explanation in the Behavioural Sciences*, Cambridge University Press, 1970.

Brown, S. C. (ed.), *Reason and Religion*, Ithaca and London, Cornell University Press, 1977.

Collins, Steven, *Selfless Persons*, Cambridge University Press,

Conze, Edward, *A Short History of Buddhism*, London, Allen and Unwin, 1980.

Coomaraswamy, Ananda, *Buddha and the Doctrine of Buddhism*, Bombay, Asia Publishing House, 1956.

Copi, I. M., *Introduction to Logic* 4th ed., New York, 1972.

Dasgupta, S., *A History of Indian Philosophy*, Cambridge University Press, 1969, Rept Motilal Banarsidass, 1975.

De Silva, Lyn, *The Problem of the Self in Buddhism and Christianity*, New York, Barnes and Noble, 1979.

De Silva, Padmasiri, *Buddhist and Freudian Psychology*, Colombo, Lake House, 1973.

De Silva, Padmasiri, *An Introduction to Buddhist Psychology*, London, 1979.

Dharmasiri, Gunapala, *A Buddhist Critique of the Christian Concept of God*, Colombo, Lake House, 1974.

Donnelly, John (ed.), *Language, Metaphysics, and Death*, New York, Fordham University Press, 1978.

Ducasse, C.J., *The Belief in a Life After Death*, Illinois, Charles C. Thomas Publishers, 1961.

Durkheim, E., *Elementary Forms of the Religious Life*, London, Allen and Unwin, 1915.

Eliade, Mircea, *Patterns in Comparative Religion*, London and New York, Sheed and Ward, 1958.

Ellis, Brian, *Rational Belief Systems*, Oxford, Basil Blackwell, 1979.

Eliot, Sir Charles, *Hinduism and Buddhism*, London, 1921.

Foster, Paul, *The Buddhist Influence in T. S. Eliot's "Four Quarters,"* Frankfurt, Haag and Herchen, 1977.

Frauwallner, Erich, *History of Buddhism* vols. I and II, Delhi, Motilal Banarsidass, 1973.

Frazer, J. G., *The Belief in Immortality and the Worship of the Dead*, London, MacMillan, 1913.

Frazer, Sir James George, *The Golden Bough*, London, Macmillan, 1936.

Gaskin, J.C.A., *Hume's Philosophy of Religion*, London, Macmillan, 1978.

Geach, Peter, *God and the Soul*, London, Routledge and Kegan Paul, 1969.

Gombrich, Richard, *Precept and Practice*, Oxford, Clarendon Press, 1971.

Gudmunsen, Chris, *Wittgenstein and Buddhism*, London, Macmillan, 1977.

Hebblethwaite, Brain and Sutherland, Steward (eds.), *The Philosophical Frontiers of Christian Theology*, Cambridge University Press, 1982.

Helm, Paul, *The Varieties of Belief*, London, Allen and Unwin, 1973.

Hick, John, *Death and Eternal Life*, London, 1976.

Hick, John, *Faith and Knowledge*, London, 1966.

Hick, John, *Faith and the Philosophers*, London, 1964.

Hudson, William, *A Philosophical Approach to Religion*, London, Macmillan, 1974.

Hudson, William (ed.), *The Is-Ought Question*, London, Macmillan, 1969.

Hume, David, *The Philosophical Works* ed. by T. H. Green and T. H. Grose in four volumes, Germany, Scientia Verlag Aalen, 1964.

Jayatilleke, K.N., *Early Buddhist Theory of Knowledge*, London, Allen and Unwin, 1963. Reprinted by Motilal Banarsidass, 1979.

Jayatilleke, K.N., *The Message of the Buddha* ed. by Ninian Smart, London, Allen and Unwin, 1975.

Johansson, Rune, *Dynamic Psychology of Early Buddhism*, London, Curzon Press, 1979.

Johansson, Rune Earl A., *The Psychology of Nirvana*, London, Allen and Unwin, 1969.

Kalupahana, David J., *Buddhist Philosophy*, Honolulu, University of Hawaii Press, 1976.

Kalupahana, David J., Causality: *The Central Philosophy of Buddhism*, Honolulu, University of Hawaii Press, 1975.

Law, B. C., *History of Pāli Literature*, London, 1933.

Lewis, H. D., *The Elusive Mind*, London, 1969.

MacIntyre, A. *Against the Self-Images of the Age*, London, Gerald Duckworth and Co. Ltd., 1971.

Marasinghe, M.M.J., *Gods in Early Buddhism*, Sri Lanka, Vidyalankara Campus Press, 1974.

Mitchell, Basil, *The Justification of Religious Belief*, London, Macmillan, 1973.

Mitchell, Basil, *The Philosophy of Religion*, Oxford University Press, 1971.

Mizuno, Kogen, *Primitive Buddhism* translated by K. Yamamoto, Japan, Karinbunko, 1969.

Moore, George Edward, *Philosophical Papers*, London, Allen and Unwin, 1959.

Murti, T.R.V., *The Central Philosophy of Buddhism*, London, 1960.

Nakamura, Hajime, *Buddhism in Comparative Light*, New Delhi, Islam and the Modern Age Society, 1975; second ed., Motilal Banarsidass, 1986.

Nanananda, *Concept and Reality in Early Buddhist Thought*, Kandy, Buddhist Publication Society, 1971.

Northrop, F.S.C., *The Meeting of East and West*, New York, 1960.

Penelhum, Terence, *Problems of Religious Knowledge*, London, Macmillan, 1971.

Penelhum, Terence, *Survival and Disembodied Existence*, London, Routledge & Kegan Paul, 1970.

Phillips, D. Z., *The Concept of Prayer*, London, 1965.

Phillips, D. Z., *Death and Immortality*, London, Macmillan, 1970.

Phillips, D. Z., *Religion Without Explanation*, Oxford, Basil Blackwell, 1976.

Potter, Karl, *Presuppositions of India's Philosophies*, New Jersey, Prentice-Hall, 1963.

Poussin, L. De la Vallee, *The Way to Nirvana*, Cambridge University Press, 1917.

Pye, Michael, *The Buddha*, London and Dallas, Duckworth, 1979.

Radhakrishnan, S. and Raju, P.T., *The Concept of Man*, London, Allen and Unwin, 1960.

Radhakrishnan, S., *Indian Philosophy* vols., I and II, London, 1929.

Rhys Davids, C.A.F., *Buddhist Psychology*, London, 1914.

Rhys Davids, C.A.F., *Indian Religion and Survival*, London, Allen and Unwin, 1934.

Rhys Davids, C.A.F., *Mind in Buddhism*, London, circa. 1934, reprinted from *Buddhism in England* vol. 9.

Rhys Davids, T.W., *Lectures on the Origin and Growth of Religion*, London, Williams and Norgate, 1906.

Ryle, Gilbert, *The Concept of Mind*, London, Penguin, 1963.

Smart, Ninian, *The Yogi and the Devotee*, London, Allen and Unwin, 1968.

Smith, Norman Kemp, *Hume's Dialogues Concerning Natural Religion*, London, Nelson and Sons, 2nd. ed., 1947.

Sogen, Yamakami, *Systems of Buddhistic Thought*, Calcutta, University of Calcutta, 1912.

Staal, J. Fritz, *Exploring Mysticism*, University of California Press, 1975.

Stcherbatsky, Th., *The Central Conception of Buddhism and the Meaning of the Word "Dharma"*, Calcutta, 1956.

Strawson, P.F., *Individuals*, London, 1959.

Sutherland, Stewart R., *God, Jesus and Belief*, Oxford, Basil Blackwell, 1984.

Sutherland, Stewart R., *Atheism and the Rejection of God*, Oxford, Basil Blackwell, 1977.

Thomas, E. J., *History of Buddhist Thought*, London, Routledge & Kegan Paul, 1971 edition.

Upadhyaya, K. N., *Early Buddhism and the Bhagavadgītā*, Delhi, Motilal Banarsidass, 1970.

Warder, A. K., *Indian Buddhism*, Delhi, Motilal Banarsidass, 1970.

Weber, Max, *The Religion of India* trans. by Gerth, H. H. and Martindale, D., New York, Free Press, 1958.

Wilson, Bryan R., *Rationality*, Oxford, Basil Blackwell, 1977.

Wittgenstein, Ludwig, *On Certainty*, ed. by Anscombe, G.E.M. and Von Wright, G. H., Oxford, Basil Blackwell, 1977.

II. *Other Sources Consulted*

Basham, A.L., 'The Rise of Buddhism in its Historical Context' in *Journal of Asian Studies*, IV, 3, Dec. 1966.

Buddhadatta, A. P., 'Who Was Buddhaghosa?' in *University of Ceylon Review*, vol. II no. 1, Nov. 1944.

Conze, Edward, 'Buddhist Philosophy and Its European Parallels' in *Philosophy East & West*, vol. XIII no. 1, Ap. 1963.

Conze, Edward, 'Spurious Parallels to Buddhist Philosophy' in *Philosophy East & West*, XIII no. 2, July 1963.

De Silva, Padmasiri, 'Doctrinal Buddhism and Healing Rituals' in *The Sri Lanka Journal of the Humanities*, vol. III nos. I and 2, 1977.

De Silva, Padmasiri, 'Schopenhauer—A Link Between the Buddha and Freud?' in *The Ceylon Journal of the Humanities*, vol. I no. 2, July 1970.

Filliozat, Jean, 'The Psychological Discoveries of Buddhism' in *University of Ceylon Review*, vol. XIII nos. 2 and 3, April-July 1955 issue.

Gombrich, Richard, 'On Being Sanskritic' A Plea for Civilized Study and the Study of Civilization, an inaugural lecture delivered before the University of Oxford on 14 October 1977, Oxford, Clarendon Press, 1978.

Hanson, A.S., 'Buddhism and Logic' in *the Middle Way*, 45, vol. XLV no. 2, London, August 1970.

Horner, I. B., 'The Basic Position of Sila', 9th lecture under the Dona Alphina Ratnayake Trust, Colombo, Lake House, 1950.

Horner, I. B., 'Early Buddhist Dhamma' in *Artibus Asiae*, XI, 1/2, Switzerland, 1948.

Jayatilleke, K. N., 'The Buddhist Attitude to Other Religions' in *University Buddhist*, Colombo, 1958.

Jayatilleke, K. N., 'Buddhist Relativity and the One World Concept' in Jurji, E. (ed.), *Religious Pluralism and World Community*, Leiden, E. J. Brill, 1969.

Jayatilleke, K. N., 'Ethics in Buddhist Perspective', Wheel Publication No. 1751176, Kandy, Buddhist Publication Society, 1972.

Jayatilleke, K.N., 'Factual Meaning and Verification' in *University of Ceylon Review*, vol. XIII no. 1, January 1955.

Jayatilleke, K. N., 'Some Problems of Translation and Interpretation II' in *University of Ceylon Review*, vol. VIII no. 1, January 1950.

Jayatilleke, K. N., 'Survival and Karma', Buddhist Publication Society, Kandy, 1969.

Jayawickrama, N. A., 'Dukkha—A Basic Concept in Buddhism' in *The Three Basic Facts of Existence*, Buddhist Publication Society, Kandy, 1973.

Johannson, Rune E.A., 'Citta, Mano, Viññāṇa—A Psychosemantic Investigation' in *University of Ceylon Review* vol. XXIII nos. 1 and 2, April 1964-October 1965 issue.

Kalansuriya, A.D.P., 'Two Modern Sinhalese Views of Nibbana' in *Religion*, vol. 9, Spring 1979.

Kalupahana, D. J. and Tamura, Kōyu, 'Antarābhava' in Malalasekera, G.P. (ed.), *Encyclopedia of Buddhism*, vol. I, Ceylon, Government Press, 1961.

Kalupahana, D. J., 'Aspects of the Buddhist Theory of the External World and the Emergence of the Philosophical Schools in Buddhism', vol. I no. 1, Jan. 1970, *Ceylon Journal of the Humanities.*

Kalupahana, D. J., 'Schools of Buddhism in Early Ceylon' in *The Ceylon Journal of the Humanities*, vol. I no. 2, July 1970.

Kunte, M. M., 'Nirvana' in *Journal of the Royal Assiatic Society Ceylon Branch*, vol. VII part III no. 25, 1882.

MacIntyre, A., 'Is Understanding Religion Compatible with Believing?' in *Faith and the Philosophers*, London, Macmillan, 1964.

Malalasekera, G.P., 'Anatta' in *Encyclopedia of Buddhism*, vol. I, Colombo, Government of Ceylon, 1961.

Malcolm, Norman, 'Postscript' in Brown, S.C. (ed.,) *Reason and Religion*, New York and London, Cornell University Press, 1977.

Maquet, Jacques, 'Expressive Space and Theravada Values: a Meditation Monastery in Sri Lanka' in *Ethos*, vol. 3 no. 1, Spring 1975.

Masefield, Peter, 'The Nibbāna-Parinibbāna Controversy' in *Religion*, vol. 9, Autumn 1979.

Matthews, Bruce, 'Notes on the Concept of the Will in Early Buddhism', in *The Sri Lanka Journal of the Humanities*, vol. 1 no. 2, December 1975.

Mitchell, Basil, 'Faith and Reason: A False Antithesis?' in *Religious Studies*, vol. 16 no. 2, June 1980.

Murti, T.R.V., 'The Two Traditions in Indian Philosophy' in *University of Ceylon Review*, vol. X no. 3, 1952.

Nanamoli Thera, 'Dukkha According to the Theravada' in *The Three Basic Facts of Existence*, Kandy, Buddhist Publication Society, 1973.

Nanananda, *The Magic of the Mind in Buddhist Perspective*, Kandy, Buddhist Publication Society, 1974.

Narada Thera, *The Buddhist Doctrine of Kamma and Rebirth*, Kandy, Union Printing Works, B. E. 2500.

Nyanaponika, *Anattā* and *Nibbāna*, Kandy, Buddhist Publication Society, 1959.

Nyanatiloka, *Karma and Rebirth*, Colombo, Colombo Apothecaries' Co. Ltd., 1947.

Obeyesekere, Gananath, 'The Goddess Pattini and the Lord Buddha: Notes on the Myth of the Birth of the Deity' *Social Compass*, XX, 1973/2.

Piyananda, Dickwela, 'The Concept of Mind in Early Buddhism', unpublished Ph.D. dissertation, Catholic University of America, 1974.

Premasiri, P. D., 'Interpretation of Two Principal Ethical Terms in Early Buddhism' in *Sri Lanka Journal of the Humanities*, vol. 2 no. 1, June 1976.

Price, H. H., 'Survival and the Idea of "Another World" ' in *Journal for the Society of Physical Research*, 37, 1953-1954; reprinted in *Brain and Mind* ed. by Smythes, London, Routledge, 1965.

Sarathchandra, 'The Basic Premises of Buddhism' in R. Tillekeratne (ed.), *University Buddhist* vol. 4, 1952-1953.

Sarathchandra, 'Bhavanga and the Buddhist Psychology of Perception' in *University of Ceylon Review*, vol. I no. 1, Ap. 1943.

Staal, J.F., 'Indian Logic, in 'Logic History of' in *Encyclopedia of Philosophy*, vol. 4, New York, Macmillan, 1967.

Staal, J.F., 'Negation and the Law of Contradiction in Indian Thought', *Bulletin of the School of Oriental and African Studies*, 25, vol. XXV, 1962.

Sutherland, Stewart R., 'Goodness and Particularity', an inaugural lecture in the Chair of the History and Philosophy of Religion delivered at University of London, King's College, on 13th February 1979.

Sutherland, Stewart R., 'Immortality and Resurrection' in *Religious Studies*, 3, 1967.

Sutherland, Stewart R., 'On the Idea of a Form of Life' in *Religious Studies*, 11, Sept. 1975.

Sutherland, Stewart R., 'St. Paul's Damascus Experience' in *Sophia*, 1975.

Sutherland, Stewart R., 'What Happens After Death?', *Scottish Journal of Theology* vol. 22 no. 4, December 1969.

Thouless, R., 'Varieties of Theories about Survival', 2nd annual Social Psychology Research Conference, March 1978.

Wittgenstein, Ludwig, 'Wittgenstein's Remarks on the Golden Bough' in *The Human World*, no. 3, May 1971.

Wijesekera, O. H. de A., 'Pali "Vado Vedeyyo" and Upanisadic "Avaki-Anadarah" 'in *University of Ceylon Review*, vol. III no. 2, Nov. 1945.

Wijesekera, O. H. de A., 'The Philosophical Import of Vedic Yakṣa and Pāli Yakkha' in *University of Ceylon Review*, vol. 1 no. 2, Nov. 1943.

Wijesekera, O. H. de A., 'Upanishadic Terms for Sense Functions' in *University of Ceylon Review*,fvol. II no. 1, Nov. 1944.

Wijesekera, O. H. de A., 'Vedic Gandharva and Pāli Gandhabba' in *University of Ceylon Review*, vol. III no. 1, 1945.

Wijesekera, O. H. de A., 'Vitalism and Becoming: A Comparative Study' in *University of Ceylon Review*, vol I no. 1, April 1943.

Winch, Peter, 'The Idea of a Social Science' in Bryan R. Wilson, *Rationality*, Oxford, Basil Blackwell, 1977.

Winch, Peter, 'Meaning and Religious Language', in S.C. Brown, *Reason and Religion*, Ithaca and London, 1977.

INDEX